JNANESHVAR:

THE LIFE AND WORKS
OF THE CELEBRATED
THIRTEENTH CENTURY
INDIAN MYSTIC-POET

Sri Garib Das Oriental Series No. 254

JNANESHVAR:

THE LIFE AND WORKS OF THE CELEBRATED THIRTEENTH CENTURY INDIAN MYSTIC-POET

S. Abhayananda

Sri Satguru Publications
A Division of
Indian Books Centre
Delhi, India

Published by
Sri Satguru Publications,
Indological and Oriental Publishers
A Division of
Indian Books Centre
40/5, Shakti Nagar,
Delhi-110007
India

Email: ibcindia@vsnl.com
Website: http://www.indianbookscentre.com

First Indian Edition; Delhi, 2000

ISBN 81-7030-674-4

Published by Sunil Gupta for Sri Satguru Publications, a division of Indian Books Centre, 40/5, Shakti Nagar, Delhi-110007, India and printed at Chawla Offset Printers, Delhi 110 052

CONTENTS

BOOK ONE:
The Life Of Jnaneshvar

BOOK TWO:
The Works Of Jnaneshvar

BOOK ONE:

The Life of Jnaneshvar

PREFACE TO BOOK ONE:
The Life Of Jnaneshvar

The story of the life of Jnaneshvar is necessarily sketchy, as many of the existing accounts of his life, written several centuries ago, are highly imaginative, to say the least. Indian hagiographers traditionally wrote about their Medieval saints as though they were celestial gods translocated to earth to appear in human guise for the benefit of suffering humanity. The story of their lives was related as a series of miraculous events from beginning to end, culminating in the saint's supernatural epiphany and resurrection in his celestial habitat. It is oftentimes very difficult, therefore, to reconstruct from such accounts a real, living, feeling, human being and to get a clear understanding of what that saint's life was really like. The life of Jnaneshvar is no exception to this rule; he is pictured in existing icons as though he were a porcelin doll, and represented in literature as a godlike being who flew about on brick walls, caused bullocks to recite the Vedas, and, at the age of twenty-five, after having left his message for mortals, released his body to return to his abode in Kailas, his celestial mountain paradise.

Fortunately, however, there are enough facts preserved from the recorded recollections of his contemporaries, and enough data available concerning the historical period in which he lived to piece together a likely story of the life and career of Jnaneshvar, who emerges as one of the most brilliant poets, sublime mystics, and facinating figures in all of Medieval Indian history. At an age when most men have scarcely begun their life's work, Jnaneshvar (*Gyan-esh-war*), who lived from 1271 to 1296, a mere span of twenty-five years, had ended his; but not before having built an everlasting monument to his memory in the written masterpieces he left behind. In so few years, he had established a legacy that was to revitalize his culture, his language, his religious tradition, and make a place for himself as an enduring presence in the hearts of his countrymen for all time.

Had the thirteenth century been blessed with no other luminary than Jnaneshvar, still it would have been a glorious century for the literature of God-knowledge; but Jnaneshvar was not the only star in the world's sky in that shining century. In Christian Europe, at the same time as Jnaneshvar, there lived a learned Prior at Erfurt, in Germany, by the name of Johann Eckhart (1260-1327) who had directly known and experienced God in mystical vision, and was embarrassing the officials of the Catholic Church by declaring before all his congregation that he had done so. Eckhart, known as Meister Eckhart, was undoubtedly the bright star in the European firmament of the thirteenth century, and the Christian equivalent of Jnaneshvar in mystical knowledge. He was only eleven years older than Jnaneshvar, and it is certainly possible that the revelation of unity which each of them experienced occurred around the same period (1288-1293). Like Jnaneshvar, Eckhart was to inspire a mystical movement with a succession of genuine mystics trailing after him, and, like Jnaneshvar, he was to revolutionize and set the standard for a budding literary language. Also, like Jnaneshvar, he was to live misunderstood, unappreciated, and persecuted during his own lifetime.

The world of Islam also had its luminaries: the great Sufi mystic-poets, Farid-uddin Attar (d. 1230), Fakhr-uddin Iraqi (d. 1289), and the incomparable Jalal-uddin Rumi (d. 1273); but it was the Spanish-Arab, Muhi-uddin Ibn al-Arabi (1165-1240), who, probably more than any other, qualifies for the position of mystical influence which Jnaneshvar and Eckhart came to hold in their respective worlds. Jnaneshvar, Eckhart and Ibn Arabi, though born in widely divergent locations and religious traditions, each experienced the revelation of cosmic Unity; and, though one called that Unity by the name of *Shiva*, and another called it *Gottheit*, and the other called it *Haqq*, the Unity which they experienced was the same, and their descriptions of it were identical.

However, the writings of Eckhart and Ibn Arabi were the products of men well into their maturity; Jnaneshvar was but a boy when he had concluded his life's work. How, we must wonder, did such profound mystical knowledge and literary genius arise in this young, casteless, peasant-boy, orphaned and living in utter poverty on the banks of the Godavari river? How is it possible that a lad of nineteen possessed the vast learning and mature wisdom to write the *Jnaneshvari* and a year later *Amritanubhav*? And why did he choose to end his life at the age of twenty-five? Why did his sister and two brothers take their own lives shortly thereafter? To these questions there will never be conclusive answers. But, in piecing together the tale of Jnaneshvar's life and times, we may find a few clues which will enable us to draw our own conclusions.

It is a tale I've chosen to tell in a somewhat unorthodox fashion, weaving together the chronicles of historical fact with the kind of recreative drama usually reserved for fictional literature. I have taken this licence as a storyteller in order to impart a sense of life and immediate drama to a tale which, because of its many diverse elements and esoteric themes, might tend to be taxing to the reader if told entirely in the usual narrative style of the historian. And while I have taken stylistic licence, I have conscientiously avoided taking licence with historical fact; all events described herein are consistent with the chronicles of historians and reliable contemporaries of Jnaneshvar.

It seems that, up to now, Jnaneshvar has not been adequately treated or appreciated in the West; and so it is my hope that this book may serve to provide that appreciation by familiarizing Western readers with this best loved poet-saint of India, and with some of his lesser known works which rightly deserve a prominent place among the world's great masterpieces of mystical literature.

Swami Abhayananda
August, 1983

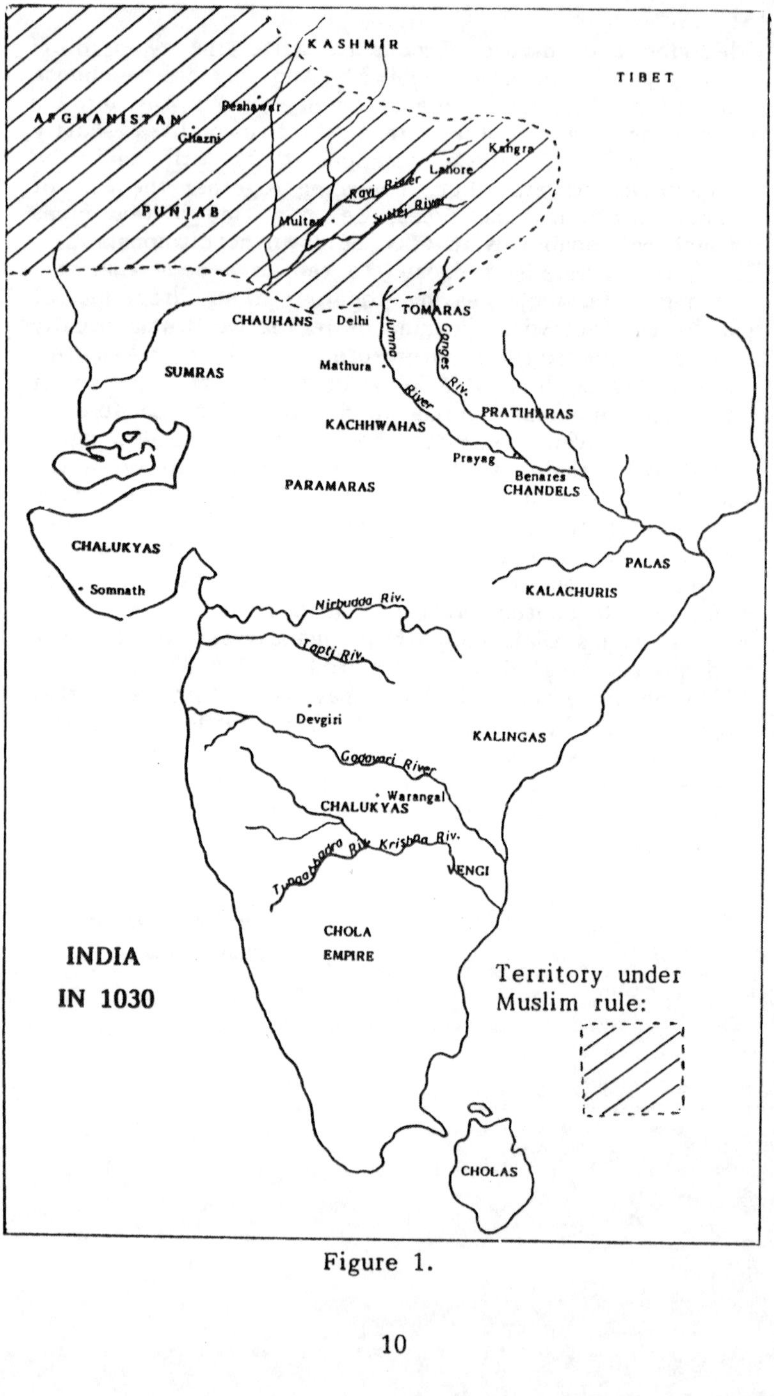
KASHMIR
TIBET
AFGHANISTAN
Peshawar
Ghazni
Kangra
Lahore
Ravi River
Sutlej River
PUNJAB
Multan
CHAUHANS
Delhi
TOMARAS
Jumna River
Ganges Riv.
SUMRAS
Mathura
PRATIHARAS
KACHHWAHAS
Prayag
Benares
CHANDELS
PARAMARAS
CHALUKYAS
Somnath
PALAS
KALACHURIS
Nirbudda Riv.
Tapti Riv.
Devgiri
KALINGAS
Godavari River
Warangal
CHALUKYAS
Tungabhadra Riv.
Krishna Riv.
VENGI
CHOLA
EMPIRE
INDIA
IN 1030
Territory under
Muslim rule:
CHOLAS

Figure 1.

1 THE HISTORICAL SETTING

The lives and works of the great cannot be viewed clearly without some understanding of the historical milieu in which such persons lived. Even a yogi and saint such as Jnaneshvar could not escape the influence of his times and the effects of his environment. Jnaneshvar's life was a perpetual drama of struggle against poverty and caste persecution, played out against a backdrop of the invasion of his country by a foreign power; for India, in the 13th century, was a land under seige.

Since the latter part of the 10th century, India and her people had been under attack by the conquering Muslims from the northwest; it was a seige which was to continue for more than five centuries. Will Durant, in his *Story Of Civilization*, calls it "probably the bloodiest story in history." And it was justified by the basic conception of the Muslim state: that all non-Muslims are its enemies and are to be slain. The holy Quran, the word of the Prophet, says: "Kill those who join other deities to Allah, wherever you shall find them. But if they shall convert ... then let them go their way." [1] And again: "Say to the infidel, if they desist from their unbelief, what is past is forgiven them. But if they return to it, ... fight then against them to the end, until the only religion left is Allah's." [2]

The Turkish ruler, Sabuktigin, was the first of a long line of Muslim princes who, finding their justification in the commands of Muhammed, and spurred by their own lust for wealth and new lands, led their conquering armies into India by the gateway of Afghanistan, which lay on her northwestern border. Making his capital at Ghazni in Afghanistan, Sabuktigin led the first holy Muslim campaigns into India's northwestern province, the Punjab, in the year 986 of our Current Era. (See the map in figure 1.)

In the following year, Sabuktigin was succeeded by his son, Mahmud, known as "the idol-breaker", who declared:

> The whole country of India is full of gold and jewels, and of the plants which grow there are those fit for making wearing-

> apparel, and aromatic plants and the sugarcane, and the whole aspect of the country is pleasant and delightful. Now since the inhabitants are chiefly infidels and idolators, by the order of God and His Prophet, it is right for us to conquer them.[3]

Mahmud's hordes of Turkish cavalry were far too many, too swift, and too skilled for the peaceful and unsuspecting Indian peoples, and he was able to push his raiding parties further and further into northern India, harvesting immense wealth from the temples containing treasures accumulated over centuries. From the city of Kangra Mahmud carried back to Ghazni "jewels and unbored pearls and rubies, shining like sparks of fire, or like iced wine; emeralds like sprigs of fresh myrtle; and diamonds the size and weight of pomegranates."[4]

In 1018 C.E., Mahmud directed his attack against the sacred city of Mathura. According to historians,

> The city was surrounded by a massive stone wall, in which were two lofty gates opening on to the river. There were magnificent temples all over the city and the largest of them stood in the center of it. The Sultan was very much struck by its grandeur. In his estimate, it cost not less than 100 million red *dinars,* and even the most skillful of masons must have taken 200 years to complete it. Among the large number of idols in the temples, five were made of pure gold, the eyes of one of them were laid with two rubies worth 100 thousand *dinars*;[5] and another had a sapphire of a very heavy weight. All these five idols yielded gold weighing 98,300 *miskals.*[6] The idols of silver numbered 200.
>
> The city is said to have been within the kingdom of the Raja of Delhi, but the Sultan captured it without meeting any opposition. He seized all the gold and silver idols and ordered his soldiers to burn all the temples to the ground. The idols

> in them were deliberately broken into pieces. The city was pillaged for 20 days, and a large number of buildings were reduced to ashes. [7]

In 1023 C.E., Mahmud stormed Somnath, the holy place of pilgrimage of the Shaivites, with 30,000 of his troops, reportedly killing 50,000 Hindus, and destroying the huge stone Shiva-lingam worshipped there. He caused it to be broken into pieces, which were then carried back to Ghazni to pave the entranceway to the Jami mosque, so that the faithful of Islam might daily trample on it.

One might wonder why the provincial Rajas of India did not gather together their forces to fight off this invader, which they could have done easily. But the Rajas seemed incapable of envisualizing at that time a united national interest that took precedence over their individual provincial interests, and incapable of relaxing their centuries-old feuds with one another long enough to unite against a common enemy. Also, the Indian people were unaccustomed to this kind of fighting. From ancient times, defence was the special task of the *kshatrya* caste, and of no other. And they fought according to an ancient chivalric code. A noted historian of the Medieval period of India points out that

> The Indian kings, all of whom accepted, at any rate in theory, the law of the Dharmashastras as inalienable, waged wars according to certain humane rules. ... War being a special privilege of the martial classes, harassment of the civilian population during military operations was considered a serious lapse from the code of honor. The high regard which all the kshatryas had for the chastity of women also ruled out abduction as an incident of war.
>
> The wars in Central Asia, on the other hand, were grim struggles for survival, for the destruction of the enemies and for appropriating their womenfolk. No code circumscribed the destructive zeal of the conqueror; no canon restrained the ruth-

> lessness of their hordes. When, therefore, Mahmud's armies swept over North India, it saw torrents of barbarians sweeping across its rich plains, burning, looting, indulging in indiscriminate massacre; raping women, destroying fair cities, burning down magnificent shrines enriched by centuries of faith; enforcing an alien religion at the point of sword; abducting thousands, forcing them into unwilling marriage or concubinage; capturing hundreds of thousands of men, women and children, to be sold as slaves in the markets of Ghazni and other Central Asian markets.[8]

After Mahmud died in 1030 C.E., India enjoyed a brief respite until the rise of Muhammed Ghori, who, in 1182, conquered Sind and the Punjab. One by one, the great Indian cities fell; Ajmir, Delhi, Benares. And in 1199, the Buddhist stronghold of Bihar was taken, most of the Buddhist monks slaughtered, and with them the last vestige of Buddhism disappeared from India. The few remaining survivors fled to Tibet where they made a new home for the teachings of the Buddha. Soon after 1200, the whole of northern India, except for Rajputana, Malwa, and part of Gujerat, was under the rule of the Muslim conquerors. Muhammed Ghori was assasinated in 1206, and his general, Kutb-ud-din Ibak, became the first Muhammedan Sultan of Delhi.

During the reign of Iltutmish (1211-1236), the *ulama*, the officials of Islamic law, made a united demand to the Sultan that the Hindus should be confronted with the Quranic injunction of 'Islam or death.' The Sultan referred the question to his *wazir*, Nizam-ul-Mulk Junnaidi, who, while concurring with the ulama's interpretation of the law, and agreeing that the Hindus should either convert to Islam or be put to death, said:

> However, at the moment, India has newly been conquered, and the Muslims are so few that they are like a sprinkle of salt amid the sands of the desert. If these orders are applied to the Hindus, it is

> possible that they might combine and a general confusion might ensue, and the Muslims would be too few in number to suppress them. Later, after a few years, when in the capital and in the regions and small towns the Muslims are well established and the troops are larger, it will be possible to give Hindus the choice of 'death or Islam.' [9]

The Sultans were therefore compelled to allow the Hindus to live as *zimmis*, or second-rate citizens, who were required to pay the *jiziya*, a poll-tax of 48, 24, and 12 silver coins for the rich, the middle class, and the poor, respectively. Only brahmins, monks, beggars, children, and the blind were exempt from it. In addition to this, Hindus were not permitted to conduct open worship, nor to teach their religion. Their testimony in court was not considered legally valid, their temples and images were frequently destroyed, their wealth confiscated, and the priests and worshippers put to death.

Iltutmish, like many of the Delhi Sultans, was a man of contradictory elements; although a strong ruler and defender of the territories under the Sultanate, he was also an aspirant to the attainment of divine Truth. One religious teacher and contemporary of Iltutmish, Minhaj-us-Siraj, said of him, "The probability is that there was never a sovereign of such exemplary faith and of such kindheartedness and reverence toward recluses, devotees, divines, and doctors of religion ever enwrapped by the mother of creation in the swaddling clothes of dominion." [10] It is said that whenever Iltutmish heard about the arrival of some saint from Central Asian lands, he went out for miles to receive him and insisted on his stay at the palace; and that he used to visit paupers, mendicants and destitutes at night under disguise in order to distribute money to them.

In 1246, Iltutmish's son, Nasir-ud-din Mahmud was named Sultan, but having little inclination toward rulership, he entrusted the affairs of the government to Balban, his Deputy of State, while he devoted himself entirely to spiritual studies and the discipline of his soul. He wore his royal robes only for public appearances; otherwise he wore only an old ragged garment, and tended to his almost constant prayers and fasts. Much of his day was spent making hand-written copies of the Quran, of which he completed two or three a year. These copies were sold in the bazaar and the Sultan subsisted mainly on their proceeds. He allowed no one to serve him but his wife, who cooked his food and performed the tasks of a maid-servant.

Nasir-ud-din's Deputy, Balban, who was very much inclined to govern, cajoled Nasir-ud-din into allowing *him* to display the royal canopy over his own head at court, and it is indicative of the consolidation of Balban's power that, when one noble snickered upon seeing the white and gold canopy over his head, he was immediately killed by two assasins with daggers. Eventually, Nasir-ud-din proved superfluous, and Balban arranged to have him eliminated by poison.

In 1265, Balban became in name what he already was in fact: the Sultan of Delhi and Emperor of India. For Balban, the Muslim saying, '*al Sultan zill Allah fi'l arz*' ("The Sultan is the shadow of God on earth") was to be taken seriously. He asserted his divine status by placing around himself a picked band of uniformed soldiers who went everywhere with him, surrounding him with their glittering sabres held at the ready. In public he never spoke to anyone, even his nobles, except through his Grand Chamberlain. Anyone approaching the throne was required to prostrate himself and kiss the throne or the Sultan's feet. And because of the Mongol invasions of Central Asia, all the refugee princes and nobles, as well as the poets and scholars, of Turkey, Persia, Arabia and Afghanistan flocked to Delhi to assemble at his richly festooned court. All this went to maintain the semblance of divinity and absolute authority which Balban intended; his extreme formality and dignified demeanor struck awe and terror into the hearts of the people and kept everyone precisely in their proper place.

Despite all this, Balban seems to have been genuinely humane and eminently just in all his dealings with those around him. He had a greatly developed sense, not only of the need for respect toward the sovereignty, but also of the moral responsibility that went with so exalted a position. He seems to have

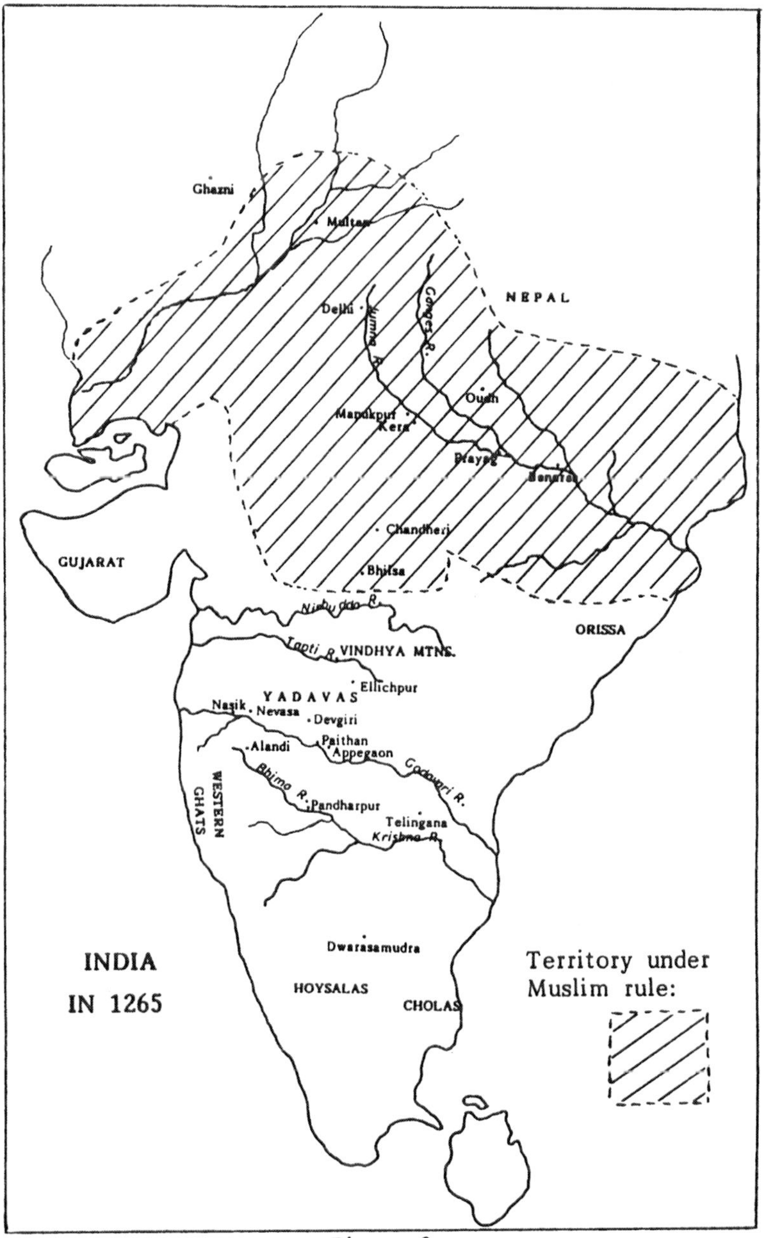

Ghazni
Multan
Delhi
Ganges R.
NEPAL
Oudh
Kera
Prayag
Chanderi
Bhilsa
GUJARAT
ORISSA
Tapti R.
VINDHYA MTNS.
Ellichpur
YADAVAS
Nasik
Nevasa
Devgiri
Alandi
Paithan
Appegaon
WESTERN GHATS
Bhima R.
Pandharpur
Telingana
Krishna R.
Dwarasamudra
HOYSALAS
CHOLAS
INDIA
IN 1265
Territory under
Muslim rule:

Figure 2.

been totally dedicated to performing his duty as 'the shadow of God', and this made of him a strong and respected leader. Though not a 'mystic' like Iltutmish or Nasir-ud-din, he had a great faith in God and in the life of virtue.

Always sober, dignified, Balban could not bear the company of "the lowborn." But he was ever-friendly toward the orthodox, respectable theologians and scholars of his day, and never failed to attend the funerals of the Shaikhs and other divines, offering consolation and stipends of money to their surviving family members.

In a speech to his son, Mahmud, he advised him to commit himself to "the protection of some holy person ... who has really renounced this world and who has dedicated himself completely to the devotion and worship of God. Beware that you never attach yourself ... to a man of the world." But, in the same speech, he showed himself above all a Muslim, saying: "Keep the infidels and idol-worshippers degraded and dishonored so that you may get a place in the company of the prophets, and crush and uproot the brahmins so that infidelity vanishes..." [11]

It was Balban's dedication to the virtues of divine sovereignty and the principles of responsible government that won for him high regard as a noble and capable ruler. During the previous reign of Sultan Iltutmish, a sort of "non-agression pact" had been established with Genghis Khan, but during Balban's reign the Mongols were again attempting in earnest to establish their strong-hold in India. Cut off from their own homeland, the Turkish Muslims of India had now to repel the Mongol hordes from the north who were breathing down their necks, and it is to the credit of Balban's foresight and strategy that it was accomplished.

The territory of India under Muslim rule at that time can be seen on the map in figure 2. It extended as far south as the Vindhya mountain range, which, because of the tremendous obstacle it presented, prevented the further encroachment of Muslim rule into southern India. The Deccan (from *Dakshinapath*, "the Southland"), bordered on the north by the Vindhyas and on the south by the Tungabhadra river, was then, as it is today, a rich lava-based plain, a fertile valley of rice and wheat producing land. The Deccan was protected from Muslim encroachment, not only on the north, but on the west and east coasts by the Ghats, the natural high-cliff barriers created by the build up of geological layers along the shores of the continent.

Here, in this bountiful plain, this peaceful oasis, unspoiled by the Muslim invaders, lay the vast Hindu kingdom of the Yadavas, ruled from the great fortessed palace at Devgiri. The kingdom of the Yadavas extended from the southern foothills of the Vindhya mountains down to the Krishna river. This vast kingdom had been ruled by the Yadava clan, said to be descended from the legendary king of Dwarka, Lord Krishna himself, since Billama Yadava seized it and declared himself king in 1191. The Yadava kings ruled from the great walled city of Devgiri, presiding over all the rural population of the towns and villages surrounding it.

It was in such a town, called Appegaon, situated on the banks of the Godavari river, only a day's ride south of Devgiri, that there lived a young brahmin named Vitthal, who was to become the father of Jnaneshvar. And, because the circumstances of Vitthal's early life were so greatly to affect those of his future son's, our story begins with the tale of Vitthal and his young wife, Rakhumabai.

2 VITTHAL AND RAKHUMABAI

In the year 1265 -- the same year that Balban was proclaimed Sultan in the north -- young Vitthal, who was then in his teens, could be seen running along the dirt road of Appegaon behind a small band of itinerant monks who had just entered the town. When these *sannyasins* passed through Appegaon, covered with ashes and carrying their begging bowls and staffs, Vitthal's mother would rush out of her house, calling out, "Vitthal! Vitthal! Come home at once! I need you here this minute!" For she knew Vitthal loved to run after the wandering *sadhus* who periodically traipsed through town in their pale orange clothes and their matted hair and beards. Vitthal loved to sit with them and listen to their mysterious talk of *Maheshvar*, the great Lord of the universe. He always brought the swamis what he could -- a few chappatis, a mango or some jack-fruit; and they allowed him to stay among them as they ate, listening with rapt attention to their stories.

Vitthal's mother knew that he would gladly go off with these monks and take up their life of wandering. But Vitthal was the son of Govinda, the *kulkarni* of Appegaon, and he also would become the headman of the village one day, with a good wife and many children. That was a good life for a man, not this good-for-nothing life of wandering, hunger, and pretentious holiness. She felt a little constriction in her heart whenever she imagined her son running off one day with these God-forsaken men.

It was just such fears which prompted Vitthal's parents to arrange for the boy's marriage to a lovely girl from the town of Alandi, the daughter of Siddhopant, who was the *kulkarni* of that town. It was a very good marriage for both children, and everyone turned out for the large wedding celebration between the two leading brahmin families of Appegaon and Alandi. Vitthal was eighteen and Rakhumabai was thirteen, a mere child, and still very much attached to her parents. Therefore, it was only natural that, immediately after their marriage, Vitthal and Rakhu went to live at the home of her parents, Siddhopant and

Kamaladev, in Alandi.

Rakhu was a good wife to Vitthal and she loved him with all her heart, but Vitthal was scarcely at home; he was always meeting with the brahmin priests at the temple, or studying the books that the priests gave him, or engaged in conversations deep into the night with whatever scholar or swami happened to be passing through town. And, in the early hours of the morning, he would arise before Rakhu awoke, and go out among the trees to meditate in the silent hours before dawn. One day, however, instead of rushing off in the morning as he usually did, Vitthal remained sitting quietly before Rakhu as she awoke. Rakhu knew immediately that he had something important to say. It was then that Vitthal told her of his decision to renounce his place in her heart and home to become a *sannyasin,* a renunciant, to study the sacred scriptures under the tutelege of a Master in Benares, to seek salvation from the sorrows of this worldly existence in meditation and prayer.

Rakhu could not believe her ears. She was to become a childless widow at the age of fourteen? What was he saying? Could he wish to leave this wonderful life in their beautiful home? She wept and pleaded with him, but finally she saw that he was not to be dissuaded. When her father heard of it, he became very angry and stalked about yelling at everyone. That night he sat up arguing with Vitthal until quite late; but Rakhu knew that it was of no use. In the morning, Vitthal put a few clothes in a cotton bag, and Rakhu, wiping the tears from her eyes, began making chappatis for him to take on his journey to Kashi, the distant holy city of Benares. "There is a great Ashram there," he told her; "that is where I am going. It is the Ashram of Ramanand Swami. If he will accept me, I will stay there as his pupil, and serve him until I have attained Brahman." He took up his bag stuffed with the chappatis and some bananas that Rakhu had put there, and, holding his palms together before his face, he made a *namaskar* to his wife, and then went off through the town toward the road that led eastward to Benares.

Rakhumabai stayed with her parents, who did their best to bring some cheer back into her life, but Rakhu had suffered a deep wound, and found it impossible to recover her gaity. She loved Vitthal, and their life together, and now she had neither Vitthal nor the children she longed to bear. She fell into dark moods of depression from which no one was able to rouse her.

As for Vitthal, he was successful in convincing Ramanand Swami of his sincere desire for God, and of his willingness to serve and to learn. As it happened, however, Swami Ramananda was just preparing a tour of some monasteries to which he had been invited as an honored guest, for he was well-known throughout the region as a holy and learned scholar and speaker. And it was not long after Vitthal had been accepted at the Ashram in Benares, and had passed through the iniation into *brahmacharya,* the preliminary to *sannyasa,* that Swami Ramananda left for his tour which led him through the cities of Prayag, Bhilsa, Devgiri, Nasik and Alandi.

In Alandi, it was the custom, when a famous or highly revered person came to town, for the family of the *kulkarni,* who was the chief official and representative of the government in the town, to enteratin and house the guest of honor in his own home. And so, when Swami Ramananda eventually reached the holy town of Alandi on the Indrayani river, he was escorted to the home of Siddhopant who, along with his entire family including Rakhumabai, were standing before their home respectfully awaiting his arrival. He was duly welcomed and shown where he could rest and refresh himself from his long journey.

At the evening meal, Swami Ramananda was given the place of honor, with Rakhu seated just opposite him. The Swami, according to custom, gave his blessings to Siddhopant's family; and to Rakhumabai, whose red-bordered sari and vermillion mark on her forehead marked her as a married woman, he said, "May your children grow to be noble and saintly examples to all the world."

Rakhu, with tears forming in her eyes, bowed her head, saying, "I pray, Swamiji, that your words could prove true, but I am childless, and Vitthal, my husband, has gone to Kashi to become a sannyasin."

"Without providing you with children?"

"Yes, sir."

"Could this be the Vitthal of Alandi who came to my Ashram just a few months ago?"

"Yes, he is my husband."

Swami Ramananda seemed to squint up his eyes, looking for some time at Rakhumabai, who was controlling her tears as best she could; then he said, "My dear, my words to you were not false; Vitthal will return to you, and you will have your children."

In the morning, as Ramanand Swami was preparing to leave for his journey home, Rakhu fell prostrate at his feet and touched his sandals. As he lifted her up, he said, "There is nothing more to cry about; you and Vitthal will produce beautiful children whose fame and glory will shine like the Sun and stir the hearts of men for all time."

Within a month's time thereafter, Vitthal returned to Alandi as his Guru had instructed him to do, and, resigned now to living the life of a householder, he took Rakhu away from her parent's home in Alandi to live in Appegaon, where he went to work for his father. There too, he earnestly set about the task of producing the children his Guru had instructed him to father.

The first child was a boy, born in 1269. So quiet and calm he was, so pure and undisturbed by even the flicker of a thought were his wide, unblinking brown eyes, that Vitthal named him Nivritti (Ni-vritt-ee), which means "without the stirring of a thought."

Two years later, in 1271, a second boy was born. This one, thought Vitthal, has the look of wisdom; his face shines with a kind of glow resembling the glow of the *jnanis*, the knowers of God. I shall call him Jnaneshvar (Gyan-esh-war), 'the Lord of knowledge.' One year thereafter, a girl was born to Vitthal and Rakhu; she was, from her very birth, independent, indrawn, aloof from everyone and everything. Though she was very beautiful, with her wispy coal-black hair and golden complexion, Vitthal felt sure she would never be snared by anyone, but would always remain pure and free. He called her Muktabai (Mook-ta-bi), 'Sister Freedom.' And, in 1273, yet another boy was born; it was Rakhu who chose the name this time. She called him Sopanadev (So-ponn-a-dev), another name for the Lord, Krishna.

3 THE NEW KING OF DEVGIRI

Only a day's ride to the north of Appegaon was the palatial city of Devgiri. And in the year of Jnaneshvar's birth, the kingdom of Devgiri saw the coronation of a new king. In 1271, Ramachandra, known affectionately by his people as Ramadeva, was crowned Raja of all the Yadava territories. Up till 1261, Ramachandra's father, Krishna Yadava, had ruled. But he had become old and infirm before Ramachandra became of age to inherit the throne, and king Krishna had appointed his own brother, Mahadev, as temporary heir to the throne at that time. Then, when Mahadev died in 1271, instead of turning the throne over to Ramachandra, who had since come of age and was the rightful heir, he appointed his own son, Amana, to the throne.

Ramachandra was enraged at his uncle's deceit, but he lacked an army of necessary strength to take the throne by force. Determined, however, to reclaim his rightful heritage, he devised a strategem: he sent a few of his soldiers into the court during the festive celebrations disguised as dancers in the musical program, and, at a signal, they took the guards by surprise. Ramachandra then captured his cousin, Amana, had him blinded, and later executed, and thus acquired the throne of Devgiri for himself.

Over the eighty years of Yadava rule, the kingdom of Devgiri had accumulated a fortune beyond imagination. Vaults full of precious stones and gold and silver in unbelievable quantities were kept in the king's possession at the palace. Some of it had been acquired by plunder; much of it from revenues collected from the territories of the vast kingdom. In the fertile Deccan plains, from the mountains in the north to the Krishna river in the south, rich crops of rice, corn, lentils, sugar cane, cotton, and spices were grown in abundance. In the city, manufacturers of brass, silver and gold articles, makers of silk and cotton cloths, artisans, builders, and architects all flourished. It was a busy city of commerce and a center of culture; and the reign of Ramachandra signalled its golden age. Architecture and the arts set new standards, wealth increased throughout the land, and the people were prosperous and content.

Ramachandra was ruler of the greatest kingdom, the most impregnable fortress, the most prized jewel of all India; and, during his long reign, he was to prove himself a just, innovative, and popular king. At the time of his coronation he won the support of the people and the religious community by building three villages of houses for 71 brahmins, and later donating a large amount of gold to the temple of Vitthala at Pandharpur for its upkeep. Jnaneshvar would later write of him: "Shri Ramachandra, the king of the universe, ruled with justice. He was the delight of the race of the Yadavas and the abode of all the arts." [12]

4 NIVRITTI FINDS HIS GURU

Despite the general prosperity of the kingdom, prospects were looking rather bleak for Vitthal and Rakhu in Appegaon. In India, to this day, when a person is excommunicated from the caste into which he was born, he is ostracized from all social contact, and deprived of his livelihood. No one will eat with him, or share water with him, or marry his children; he is avoided by everyone, pointed at with scorn, and regarded even by the people of the lowest castes as an untouchable, an outcast. Such a sentence was passed upon Vitthal by the chief brahmins of Appegaon.

Vitthal, they said, had voluntarily abandoned his brahmin caste when he submitted to the *brahmacharya* initiation, during which the sacred thread of the brahmin caste was cut along with the tuft of hair on the crown of the head significant of his caste. According to the *Dharmashastras*, the laws of caste, by his return to the life of a householder, Vitthal had sacrificed his *brahmacharya* status as well. He was now an outcaste, and his children were also outcastes.

Vitthal protested this decision, but to no avail. And when Nivritti, his eldest son, reached the age of eight, and it was time for his *upanayana*, the ceremony for the investiture of the sacred thread of the brahmins, the brahmin priests of Appegaon refused to perform it. However, Vitthal knew a brahmin priest from Alandi who now lived in Nasik, and who was aware of the strange circumstances whereby he had returned to his family at the direction of his Guru; and this priest, sympathetic to Vitthal's plight, had consented to perform the sacred thread ceremony for his son.

So, while Rakhu remained at home with the younger children, Vitthal set out with Nivritti on foot to the city of Nasik. Nasik, known as the Kashi of western India, for its many ancient and holy temples, lies, like Appegaon, on the banks of the Godavari river. Appegaon is a small village near Paithan, and Nasik is just 25 miles northwest of Appegaon, along a narrow dusty road, scarcely more than a path, which, at that time, made its way through a deep lush jungle teeming with parrots and mynah birds, monkeys, hyenas, elephants and tigers.

Starting early in the morning, Vitthal and Nivritti made it to Nasik by evening, and the investiture ceremony was performed on the following day. The ceremony itself did not take long, and Nivritti understood none of it, as the priest chanted in Sanskrit throughout. There were a few balls of rice offered to his ancestors, a sip from a bitter drink, more chanting in Sanskrit, parts of which Nivritti was asked to repeat, and the double thread was placed over his left shoulder. Vitthal paid the priest, and they made their namaskars to the priest's small *murti* of Shiva, and then departed.

On their return journey, they made a stop at a small village along the way, called Nevasa. Vitthal had purchased a coconut in Nasik, which he now offered at the foot of a small *murti* in the square Devi temple facing the road on the outskirts of town. Then, taking Nivritti's hand, Vitthal led him to the small monastery building behind the temple. There, standing with two children, four or five years old, was a kindly-faced man of middle age wearing an ochre *lunghi* wrapped about his waist. As the man saw Vitthal, his eyes lit up in recognition; turning toward him, he brought his hands together before his face, making a namaskar. "Vitthal!" the man called warmly.

"Om namo Narayanaya!" said Vitthal, returning the salutation. The man clasped Vitthal to his bare chest; "How are you, Vitthalji?"

"I'm very well, Swamiji," Vitthal laughed. "I'd like you to meet my eldest son, Nivritti." Nivritti bowed his head and made his namaskar to the Swami. "This," said Vitthal, "is Swami Satchidananda; he is an old friend."

"Ah, what a handsome boy, Vitthal!" said the Swami, appraising Nivritti; "and intelligent too, is he not?"

"Indeed he is," Vitthal replied proudly; "and I have three more at home just as handsome and just as intelligent."

"Four! Ah, Vitthal, has it been so long since we parted at Kashi?"

"It is nearly nine years," said Vitthal.

The Swami turned to the small children pulling at his legs; "These," he said, "are *my* children -- at least for the day. While their parents work in the fields, I care for the little rascals."

Nivritti and the children had been sizing up each other; now the little ones, giggling, ran off toward the rear of the monastery building. "Go along with them, Nivritti," Vitthal said, patting the boy's back; "the Swami and I would like to talk." Nivritti ran after the giggling children, while the Swami led Vitthal inside the monastery.

A little while later, the Swami had prepared a lunch for his guests, and they all sat down to a dish of rice, dal (a thick lentil soup), chappatis, and a bit of mango pickle. Nivritti listened while his father and the Swami spoke of their days together at the Ashram of Ramananda, and when they had finished their lunch and washed their mouths, Vitthal told the Swami that they would have to leave right away if they were to make it home by nightfall. And so they made their farewells to the Swami and to Nevasa, and started out once again on their journey home.

For Nivritti, the long trek through stretches of wilderness was a great adventure, as wondrous as the visit to Nasik with its many beautiful temples and endless streets; but as the day wore on, he saw only the monotonous dusty road before him, and his father had to call him repeatedly to hasten his steps. Vitthal was well aware of the dangers of the jungle after nightfall, and though they were yet far from home, darkness had already begun to fall.

All at once, a tiger appeared in the path before them. Vitthal shouted behind him, "Run, Nivritti! Run into the forest!" Nivritti ran and kept on running, blindly past trees and then up a rocky slope to a place between two large rocks where he could hide. And as he crawled into what looked like a crevice, he found himself entering a large cave. Just then, the shadowy figure of a man sitting inside the cave lifted up its head, and, showing a large delightful grin, raised a hand in salutation to Nivritti. "Come in, my boy," the man said; "don't be frightened."

Nivritti crouched just inside the cave, breathlessly, while the man inside produced a flame, seemingly from nowhere, and passed the flame to a candle nearby. In the growing light Nivritti could see the man was huge;

he was a powerfully built man with a large belly, but his face was so gentle, so like a child in its radiant delight, that Nivritti could not feel afraid. The man sat on a deerskin, wearing nothing at all on his body. Nivritti recognized by his beard and high-piled hair that he was one of the holy men such as those his father had pointed out to him in Nasik. The man cocked his head to one side and smiled so lovingly that Nivritti thought he had never seen such a kindly looking man. Then, the man motioned for Nivritti to come forward and take a seat before him. Nivritti moved cautiously.

"What brings you to my cave, my son?" the man asked.

"A tiger chased me." Nivritti said in a weak voice.

"A tiger? Really?" The man shook with laughter. "Well,, he won't bother you here. You're welcome to stay the night if you like."

"But my father will be worried," said Nivritti. And he told the man of his journey with his father to Nasik, and how they were just on the way home to Appegaon. After hearing his tale, the man thought for a moment, then said, "It's dark now in the jungle; I'll take you to your village in the morning. For tonight, you can remain here. Will that be alright?"

Nivritti wanted very much to stay in the cave; "Yes, sir; I would like to stay," he said. He knew somehow that his father was alright and that it was right for him to stay. There was a magical something about the cave and the man that attracted and also puzzled Nivriti. He had never known such a pleasant atmosphere, nor such an inner gladness, as he had experienced since entering the cave. What magical world had he stumbled upon? Who was this man for whom he felt such affection? "Who are you?" he asked the man.

"My name is Gahininath," he said in his low, pleasant voice.

"Are you a yogi?" Nivritti asked. It was a word his father had used when he pointed out the wandering holy men to him. Again Gahininath laughed, while his belly shook. Nivritti couldn't help smiling himself.

"I am a Nath. My Guru is Gorakhnath, and his Guru was Matsyendranath. We are yogis, yes. And you, too, are a yogi; and I am your Guru. Do you understand?"

Nivritti looked at Gahini's eyes, and again, he wore that look of sweet care and tender love that he had seen before; but now, it seemed two rays of shimmering light shone from the yogi's eyes into Nivritti's own, entering deep into his very soul and awakening in Nivritti a feeling he had never known before. There was, for a moment, a trembling within, like fear, and then it was gone, and he felt light as a feather and exhilarated, happy. Gahininath's hand floated out gently and rested cooly on his brow, and Nivritti was flooded with memories of this very same scene, but from long, long ago. Something altogether unexpected was happening to him; he remembered that this cave was his home, this man his dearest friend. Heavenly joys came flooding into his heart and he could not hold back the tears which burst forth as though a river had been unleashed behind his eyes.

Nivritti lay for some while, curled up on the ground. He had been riding high on the shoulders of Gahini, high on a mountain top, while purple clouds swirled around them and bolts of lightning split the skies. He remembered the brilliant light, so lovely, so cool and ... Gahininath was bending over him now, covering him with a soft tigerskin. Nivritti turned on his side and closed his eyes.

II

Dawn was just streaking the sky with lavender and gold when Jnaneshvar, returning from the well with a jug of water, saw his brother running up the path to their home. "Father! Father!" Jnaneshvar shouted; "it's Nivritti!" And, as both Vitthal and Rakhu rushed out of the house, Nivritti ran toward them, and hugged his mother around the waist.

"Where on earth have you been? We've been up the whole night searching for you!" his father demanded.

"Father, ... I ran and ran and climbed into a big cave."

"Well, thank God, you're alright!" exclaimed Rakhu. "I searched and shouted half the night and was just preparing to start out again ..."Vitthal put in; but just then he saw the huge half-naked yogi standing in the path before him.

"Father," said Nivritti, proudly, "this is Gahini; he brought me back. He lives in the cave I found."

Vitthal went forward at once, bowing to touch the toes of Gahininath and then raise his fingers to his forehead. "You are Gahini, the famous yogi of the Natha lineage?"

Yes, father," said Gahini in a voice so sweet that Rakhu, who had been holding her breath in fear now expelled it, and came forward to touch his feet also.

"This is my wife, Rakhumabai," said Vitthal; "we are very grateful to you for bringing Nivritti back to us, Yogiji. May we offer you something to drink? Please honor us by taking a little tea with us." Vitthal led the way inside, while Rakhu scrambled to prepare a hot tea for Gahininath.

As they sat and talked, Vitthal related to the yogi, Gahini, the story of his discipleship to Ramanand Swami, and his subsequent return to Appegaon. Nivritti and Jnandev respectfully remained outside with the younger children, Muktabai and Sopan, but they leaned close to the window, listening to the conversation between their father and Gahininath. Then Nivritti heard Gahini say, "Nivritti is an exceptional child: I have offered to become his Guru. Will you allow him to visit me on occasion?" There was a moment of silence. Rakhu, stirring a sweet *kheer* over the fire, stopped, holding her breath once more.

"It would be a great honor to our family," said Vitthal, "if you would serve as Guru to Nivritti. He may visit you whenever you wish."

Outside the window, Nivritti hugged Jnandev, and jumped up and down with him, allowing a little squeal of delight to pass his lips. Then, rushing back to the window, he listened once more, as Vitthal asked, "Will you honor his brother, Jnandev, also with your grace, Maharaj?" Again, Rakhu stopped her stirring, and her eyes began to blink nervously.

"How old is the boy," asked Gahininath.

When Vitthal told him, "Six years," Gahini smiled, and let out a deep "Hmmm." Then he said, "Let Nivritti be his Guru. I will teach Nivritti and Nivritti can teach your Jnandev."

"As you wish," said Vitthal; and he was greatly pleased. Rakhu stopped blinking, and brought the *kheer* (a sweet porridge) in bowls, placing one before the yogi, and one before her husband. Outside the window,

Nivritti and Jnaneshvar danced 'round and 'round, holding each other in a brotherly embrace.

5 THE DEATH OF VITTHAL

Since their trip to Nasik, Vitthal noticed, the men of the village were even more determined to scorn him and his family. They were resentful of the fact that he had gone to another town and obtained for his son the ceremony of the sacred thread despite their decision, and regarded his refusal to acquiesce to the judgement of the brahmin elders of Appegaon as an insult and grave offence. Recently, Vitthal's father had reluctantly announced to him that he could no longer allow him to work for him, for the brahmins had pronounced against it, and nearly all of the people of the village were refusing to deal with him. Vitthal now had no work as a brahmin, for in the eyes of the people he was no longer a brahmin; and neither could he claim any other caste as his own. Soon there was no food; Vitthal was forced to ask his own father and the father of Rakhu for charitable assistance.

But this was not the worst of it; because he had obeyed his master, Swami Ramananda, his wife and the children were now branded with untouchability. No other villagers or children would come near them; even the lowcaste children, such as the cobbler's children and even those of the sweepers, jeered at them, often throwing cow dung at the younger ones. Nivritti and Jnandev seemed not to mind so much the unfriendliness of their peers; they were far too preoccupied with their yoga and with their excursations into the forest to notice. But Vitthal knew that, as they grew older, this anathema would become more painful; they would find no way to live among the people of Appegaon. It was all his fault -- he was a millstone about their necks, depriving them of any chance for even a little happiness in this life. Such were the thoughts in Vitthal's mind as he slowly went one morning down the path to the river to bathe.

Jnaneshvar and Nivritti, however, were unaware of their father's distress, and of the torment he felt over the prospect of his children's future. They scarcely paid any attention to the nasty pranks of the other children of the village, and were only vaguely aware that something was amiss. It was only when they went to the temple to bow to the statue of the Devi, the Goddess, that they felt most strongly the strange unwarranted rancor of others toward them, for the priest would not allow them to enter as they had before, and he had shouted at them, calling them *mlecchas*.

But they were so engrossed in their *sadhana*, their spiritual practices, that they scarcely gave a thought to the strange behavior of the villagers. Once a week, sometimes twice a week, Nivritti went to see Gahininath in his cave in the jungle. There he would stay for the whole day, while Gahini taught him, not from books, but from the store of his accumulated knowledge and experience. Nivritti learned of the various postures and exercises for the purification of the nerves, to better enable him to meditate. He learned how to sit for long periods in the *vajrasana* posture, with his back straight, and his gaze indrawn. And he learned to hold his mind fixed on the *mantram* Gahini had taught him to use as a means of stilling and focusing his thoughts.

Then, after their meditation together, Gahini would tell Nivritti stories from the ancient yogic scriptures or from his own experience in his youthful travels. He told him about Krishna and his teachings in the *Gita*; he told him of the ancient sages, like Yajnavalkya and Ashtavakrya who lived even before Rama and the wicked Ravana. And, above all, he taught him to love God above everything, and to understand His ways, seeing Him in every creature and in everything that appeared on earth.

For the rest of the week, Nivritti became Guru to Jnaneshvar. In the early mornings, long before the Sun came up, they would sit together, meditating in stillness on the glimmering light that shone within them. And then, after their morning tea, they'd run off to a secret spot in the forest where they would practice their yogic exercises, and where, later, Jnaneshvar would listen raptly to the stories and teachings Nivritti passed on to him. And there they were, in this beautiful secret spot, deep in the green jungle, when their father's lifeless body, dripping with water, was carried by the villagers up the path to his house, where Rakhu stood speechless and horrified, with one hand over her mouth and the other clutching her bosom.

6 A NEW BEGINNING

In 1287, Rakhu also passed away. Since her husband's death, Rakhu had become progressively weaker, and when the fever epidemic hit Appegaon, she caught it and seemed to just give up, dying two days later. The children were now orphans, remaining temporarily in the care of their paternal grandparents.

Nivritti was now eighteen; Jnandev was sixteen, and Muktabai and Sopan were fifteen and fourteen respectively. They were exceedingly handsome, each one of them. Nivritti, a Capricorn, was tall, lean and strong. In demeanor, he was sober and austere; he was a yogi. Nivritti's mind was continually engrossed in contemplation, continually discriminating between the eternal and the non-eternal. When someone spoke to him, he looked at them through half-closed eyes, as though struggling to see through the appearance to the eternal reality beyond. He was very strict with himself, and followed an austere discipline; giving little time to frivolity, he could be rude to those who attempted to draw him into it.

Jnaneshvar, on the other hand, was of a devotional type, drawn to the worship of God in some form or other. He was a Leo, and greatly attracted to the idealized stories of the gods and goddesses who walked the land long, long ago, such as Rama and Krishna. His was the vision of the poet, the lover, and his only discipline was to see everything before him as a manifestation of God. He had transferred much of his devotion to Nivritti whom he regarded as his divinely appointed Guru; though he was also his brother, Nivritti had become, in Jnaneshvar's eyes, a very special manifestation of God, a divine personage who was to be worshipped and served as the Lord Himself.

Muktabai, a Piscean, was deep as the ocean and beautiful as a young goddess. Her dark, luxuriant, tresses haloed a face of angelic beauty, yet she was always modest and unassuming. She had a quiet, confident air about her even at so young an age, and her one desire and religious practice was to serve her brothers in whatever way she could. Muktabai was their cook, maid, nurse and confidant; and this was the means of her adoration and the practice of her devotion to God.

Sopan, the youngest, was a Cancer. He was a boy of many moods, and though he idolized his brothers and wished he could be more like them, he was often swayed by irresistable moods which caused him to become confused and distracted. This often resulted in some wild fit of rebellion, followed by a deep sense of sorrow and guilt that pitched him into a prolonged period of silent withdrawal. He found he could best control this wild vacillation of mood by following Muktabai's lead, remaining silent, and giving himself generously in humble service.

Since Vitthal's death, the attitude of the villagers toward the children had not changed. They were still regarded as casteless, illegitimate. And now that Rakhu was also gone, Nivritti had become the head of the family, and was expected to provide for the welfare of all. And he recognized that it was clearly time to do whatever could be done to restore the brahmin status of the family. It was decided, therefore, that Nivritti and Jnandev would go into the town of Paithan, a few miles away, and petition the pandits there to give them a letter certifying to their purity and to their membership in the brahmin caste. There was much at stake. With such a letter, they could go elsewhere, where their father's infractions were unknown, and they could begin anew. They would be able to secure positions as priests or teachers, and Muktabai would be eligible to marry if she so chose.

But Nivritti would do nothing until he had spoken to Gahininath; with Gahini's blessing, their endeavor could not fail; without it, it was a matter of great uncertainty. One month after Rakhu's body had been cremated, Nivritti went to see Gahininath. When he arrived, he found Gahini lounging outside the cave with several young disciples sitting around him. Nivritti approached and knelt to his knees before his Guru, taking the dust from his feet and touching it to his forehead. Gahini smiled happily at his disciple and motioned for him to sit alongside the others. "I was just speaking of my plans to travel south," he said. "Govinda will accompany me and Nityananda will remain in my cave while I am gone."

Nivritti suddenly realized that a great change was about to occur in his life; some unavoidable destiny was depriving him, not only of his mother, but of his Guru as well. "And when will you be returning, Babaji?" he asked as calmly as he could.

Gahini wagged his head, noncommitally. He looked at Nivritti for a long time with that stern concentrated gaze that Nivritti knew so well -- a searching gaze that went deep into his soul, beyond the boundaries of shifting time. Then Gahini rose suddenly from his seat, and beckoned Nivritti to follow him. He walked along the path that led to the roadway, and when they reached it, he took Nivritti's hand in his own. "I am going to visit many places, ..." he said; "who knows when I will come back to this place. You -- you have many responsibilities now, do you not?"

"Yes, Gurudev."

They walked on now, slowly, hand in hand. Gahini spoke again; "It would be good, Nivritti, if you could clear up this family problem. Go to Paithan; talk to the brahmin pandits there. Ask them to grant you a certificate of caste. Then you should take your family to Nasik. Yes, to Nasik. Everything will be fine."

Gahini had never before offered directions to him regarding his worldly life, and Nivritti knew that his Guru's words carried the power of destiny, and were unfailing in their blessing. Tears were now beginning to blur Nivritti's vision; "Am I never to see you again, Guruji?" he asked in a wavering voice.

Gahini patted the hand of Nivritti, then hugged him to his chest. "Of course you will. Do you think I will ever leave you?" Then he took Nivritti by the shoulders at arms length, looking knowingly and lovingly into his eyes; "Go now," he said, "and do as I've said. Everything will be fine; you and your family will be taken care of. God will bless you."

Nivritti brought his hands together before him and made *namaskar* to his Guru. A bitter lump was growing in his throat and tears were beginning to flood his eyes.

"Go on, now," Gahini said, motioning him away with a swishing motion of his hand. And as Nivritti turned and disappeared down the roadway, Gahini whispered, "God will bless you, my son."

Paithan is a very ancient and holy city, located on the north bank of the Godavari. During the time of Ptolemy, it was called Baithan, and served as the capital of the Satavahana kings. Now, it was just another busy town, a center of commerce, where one could buy bolts of silk and cotton, fine brassware, leather goods, and foodstuffs of every variety. It was also a town of many historic temples, and it was the home of a number of itinerant holy-men, Gurus, and pandits. Two such pandits were Hemopanth and Bapudev. They were the accepted authorities on the *Dharmashastras*, the laws of correct conduct and caste restrictions. Therefore, it was to them that Nivritti and Jnandev went one morning to obtain a letter of certification.

After inquiring in several temples, they found the establishment of these pandits in a room behind a textile and clothing store, and entered. "Revered sirs," Nivritti began, addressing the two stout men who sat on the floor at their low desks, "my name is Nivritti, son of the late Vitthalpanth of Appegaon, and this is my brother, Jnaneshvar. We would like to speak with you if we may on a matter requiring your expert and learned judgement."

"You are a brahmin? one of the men asked.

"Yes, sir; of the family of the *kulkarnis* of Appegaon."

"Yet your brother does not wear the sacred thread?" the man challenged.

"It is just that I wish to speak to you about, sir."

"Very well," the pandit said, pushing aside his papers; "Be seated. Tell me what is on your mind."

Nivritti and Jnaneshvar took their places on the floor before the two pandits. "My father," said Nivritti, "many years ago went to Benares, where he was initiated by a Swami ..."

"Wait!" interrupted the other pandit, who had been silent till then; "You are the children of that married Swami of Appegaon!" Turning now to the other man, he said, "You remember, the one who changed his mind after taking vows of renunciation, and then went back to his wife and had a flock of children ..."

"Sir," Nivritti interposed, "my father was asked by his Guru to return; it was beyond his decision. Besides, he has been dead now for ten years, and his deeds have died with him. Whether they were good or bad, only God can judge. My brother and I are not here to plead for him nor to ask for any judgement concerning him; we are here to ask that you grant us a letter of certification, so that my family may be free of this stigma."

"Your mother...?"

"She died over a month ago. There is only myself, Jnaneshvar, and two others -- a brother and a sister. We are staying with our grandparents, but we are a burden to them. Since we are considered outcastes, we are unable to earn any money to assist them, and because of us, they are treated badly by the community.

"We feel, sir, that we have committed no sin, that we are guiltless; yet because of our father's obedience to the command of his Guru, we are regarded as unclean. If we are granted, sir, a certificate from the hands of such respected pandits as yourselves, we shall be able to seek employment in Nasik and thus provide for our family. Otherwise, I do not see how we can survive."

The two men sat quietly for a moment, considering what the boy had said. Then one of the pandits spoke up. "How would you gain employment? Have you any learning?"

"Yes, sir," Nivritti answered; "I -- and my brother as well -- have studied the *Srutis* and the *Smritis* also, and we are proficient in the writing of Sanskrit."

"Indeed!" one of the pandits exclaimed. "And who taught you so much?"

"Sir, I have learned everything from my Guru, Sri Gahininath," answered Nivritti.

"The yogi?"

"Yes, sir."

"And you, young man," the pandit said, eyeing Jnaneshvar, "do you also claim to be learned in the *Srutis* and the *Smritis*?"

"Sir, said Jnandev, "I am not nearly so well learned as my brother."

"Yet you call yourself 'the Lord of knowledge'!"

"Sir, it is my firm conviction that all of us, including the birds and animals, are manifestations of the Lord of knowledge."

"Oh, it is, is it?" the pandit chuckled; and, spying outside his window a passing buffalo pulling a cart, he said, "And I suppose then that we should call that buffalo 'Jnaneshvar' also?"

"Sir, if you'll pardon me," said Jnandev, "I will remind you that Krishna told Arjuna, 'No being either moving or unmoving, can ever be apart from me... I am the beginning, middle and end of all that lives.' Sir, he said that in the tenth chapter of the *Gita*. And in the eleventh book of *Srimad Bhagavatam*, the Lord said to Uddhava, 'O Uddhava, this whole universe exists in me and is an expression of my divine power.' 'Therefore,' he said, 'learn to look with an equal eye upon all beings, seeing the one Self in all.' I regard this as the truest of truths, sir, and I am certain that even that buffalo is a manifestation of the one Self, the Lord of the universe, and is as worthy of the name of 'Jnaneshvar' as I am."

The two pandits sat quietly and thoughtfully. With a glance at the other for confirmation, one of them drew out a parchment and spread it on his desk. "I will give you your certificate," he said, "but there is a penance which each of you are required to observe for the remainder of your lives. Whenever you observe a man, woman, or child, a dog, pig, horse, ass or buffalo, or even a bird in the sky, you are to make obeisance to it in your heart as you would to the Lord of the universe. Do you understand?"

"Yes, sir!" both Nivritti and Jnaneshvar answered in unison.

"And do you agree?"

"Yes, sir," they answered once again; and then they fell to their knees at once, and bowed to both the pandits, touching their heads to the floor and saluting them with genuine love and gratitude.

The pandit wrote out the letter, confirming and certifying their brahmin status, signed it, and placed on it his seal. Then he passed it to the other man who added his signature and seal beneath. "You are brahmins in the eyes of man and God," he said, handing the parchment to Nivritti. "When you get to Nasik, present this to the council of elders there, and I'm sure they will help you to find some employment and will assist you in every way."

"You are truly instruments of the mercy of God," said Nivritti; "may He keep you in His care, and bestow on you His grace." The boys and the pandits saluted each other with great affection, and then the boys departed, eager to return home with their wonderful news.

The two brahmin pandits remained unable to work for some time; though each pretended to work on some document before him, neither could see for the moisture that clouded their vision. Finally, each simultaneously sat back against their cushions, and gave out a sigh.

II

With their few possessions in cloth bags on their backs, the four youngsters set out early one morning on the road to Nasik. It was a longer journey than the one Nivritti had taken with his father many years ago, because they needed to stop often to rest from the burdens they carried. It was late, and the Sun had already set below the horizon when they arrived at the junction of the Pravara and Godavari rivers. Nivritti recalled that the monastery of Nevasa was just a short way from there. "We'll stop at the monastery of Swami Satchidananda," he told the others; "we should be able to spend the night there."

When they arrived, it was nearly dark, but they could see no light in the small *kutir* of the monastery. "Perhaps it's deserted," Jnaneshvar said, when no one answered their knock. Nivritti tried the door, and finding it open, led the way inside. There was no one at home; but there were several mats on the floor for sleeping, and to one side a small cookstove with a chimney. "We'll sleep here tonight," said Nivritti to the others; "bring everything inside."

Jnandev found a tinder box on the cookstove hearth, and told Sopan to gather some sticks outside for a fire. Nivritti, still exploring the monastery, went to a door at the rear and peered into a small dark room. "Jnandev!" he shouted, "come here!" and he disappeared into the room. When Jnaneshvar entered, he saw a man lying on a mat on the floor with Nivritti kneeling over him. "It's the Swami," Nivritti said; he's sick!"

They soon had a tallow candle burning and were able to see more clearly. The Swami was occasionally conscious, but he was delerious with fever. Nivritti stayed with him, holding him, while Jnandev managed to get a fire going in the cook stove. Sopan went for water, while Muktabai rummaged in their bags for her herbs and cooking utensils.

The boys rinsed the Swami's face and brow with cool water, and Muktabai prepared a soup of thick rice broth and herbs. Sitting him up, they managed to get him to swallow some of the hot liquid. When he would take no more, they laid him down and covered him well with some of the clothing which they had brought with them. And then they too took some nourishment of rice and cold chappatis which they had brought with them.

Though the Swami's fever seemed to have broken and he was sleeping peacefully, Jnandev thought it best to remain with him through the night, and so he spread his mat in the back room alongside the Swami, while the others, exhausted from their long journey, made their beds in the larger room.

In the morning, the Swami was given more of the hot broth, while Sopan was sent into the village to purchase some milk. The Swami seemed to be reviving now, and Nivritti and Jnandev watched over him, sooth-him and keeping him covered and warm. When Sopan returned with the milk, Muktabai warmed it and made a milk tea which seemed to have a very good effect on the Swami. He sat there, looking around at the children hovering over him so solicitously. "Who are you?" he finally managed to ask.

"Don't you remember me?" said Nivritti; "my name is Nivritti -- I came here once with my father, Vitthal from Appegaon, many years ago. And these are my brothers and sister."

"Nivritti ... yes, of course, I remember...," the Swami said. "Where is your father?"

"He died quite a few years ago, Swamiji."

"I'm sorry...," he said.

"This is Jnaneshvar; he stayed in here with you

last night. And this is Muktabai, and this is Sopan," said Nivritti, pulling each of them forward in turn. "We were on our way to Nasik, and since it was getting late, we stopped here for the night."

"I'm very glad you did," said the Swami. "I've been alone here for quite some time, and I haven't been feeling very well..."

"Just rest," said Jnandev.

Muktabai spoke from the doorway, "If you think you could eat something solid, Swamiji, I will bring you some rice."

"Yes, ... I think so," the Swami replied. And they knew then that he was going to be alright.

In the next few days, the Swami gradually regained his strength, and was moving about slowly on his own. Muktabai cooked chappatis and rice and dal for him and brought him ginger tea in the mornings. She and Sopan attacked the monastery with brooms and cleaned it out, and aired the bedding and washed the Swami's clothes in the river and laid them out in the Sun to dry.

Nivritti and Jnandev had gone to Nasik, which was only a short distance away, and had spoken with some of the council elders and had shown them the letter of certification from the pandits of Paithan, but the brahmins were wary and suspicious. There was no work for them just now, they said; there were already too many young brahmins around seeking work as priests and assistants. Nivritti and Jnandev returned to the monastery in rather low spirits after traipsing around Nasik all day. They had inquired at all the temples and schools, and received the same answer from everyone. That evening, after their dinner, they sat outside in the cool night air with the Swami, and recounted to him the unencouraging results of their day long search.

"Why not stay here!" the Swami said, after listening to their story.

"You are very kind, Swamiji," said Jnandev, "and we are very grateful for your hospitality, but ..."

"Now listen," the Swami interrupted; "you youngsters need a place to stay; I need the company. Besides, there's going to be plenty to do around here now that warm weather's on the way. There'll be many people stopping here, wanting something to eat, and parents wanting to leave their children here with me. We'll have a little school here. We'll have plenty to eat; the elders bring food for the orphans, and there's a huge mango orchard out back, and we can put in some corn and peppers in the field ... What do you say? Please say you'll stay. I would love for you all to stay!"

The children looked around at one another. Finally Jnaneshvar said, "Well, if you still want us to stay even after tasting Mukti's cooking, then I guess you've got it coming." And they all laughed, as Muktabai squealed and pretended to pull at Jnandev's hair. It was decided; they had a new home -- one in which they would remain for six wonderful years of their lives.

7 JNANESHVAR BECOMES ENLIGHTENED

They were quiet years for the children from Appegaon; Jnandev and Nivritti grew into manhood, Muktabai became a living goddess of beauty and grace, and Sopan became strong in body and mind. Satchidananda had never in his life been so happy as he was with his newly adopted family; and now that they were free to devote themselves entirely to their sadhana, their search for God, all the children had become filled with knowledge and light. People from nearby villages had begun making pilgrimages to Nevasa to visit the little monastery where the young yogis dwelt, and there was always a cheerful welcome from the Swami, and a ready cup of tea and a smile from the lovely Muktabai. If someone needed solace or advice, they would come and talk with any one of the children or the Swami, and would leave refreshed, with their faith and confidence restored. Some came just to spend some time in the holy and peaceful atmosphere of the monastery and temple grounds; this, by itself, seemed to answer their questions and resolve their confusion.

There was always enough to eat and enough to provide for necessities. Those who came usually brought a little gift for the monastery -- a basket of fruit, a bag of flour, a cocoanut; and there was always plenty to share, as more and more of the townspeople came to know of the rare family of orphans and the good Swami who lived in the little monastery.

Sopan was responsible for keeping the place clean and beautiful; but his greatest interest was in tending the orchard and the small garden which he created in back of the monastery. He grew ginger-root and red peppers for spice; and some yellow corn, okra and squash as well. He seemed never to tire of working, and never to be quite at ease unless he was. He was a true *karma-yogin*, entirely devoted to the service of God in the form of his family and the others who came to Nevasa. He had found his own way to be very happy; and all who saw him remarked how cheerful and sweet he always seemed, how happy and fulfilled.

Muktabai had now entered those years when most young girls become vain, impertinent and flirtatious; but

Mukti was no ordinary girl. She was entirely self-possessed, always considerate, gracious, and never presumptuous. The truth is that she simply had no interest in the prospect of marriage or in any kind of familiarity which would take her mind from the joy she felt in the love and service of God. She longed to merge, like Radha, with the adorable Krishna; she longed to serve chastely, like Sita, the divine Rama. Yet she truly felt just as fortunate and blessed as Radha or Sita in her role as sister, friend, and servant to her divine brothers, who seemed to her the very incarnation of Rama and Krishna in this world. She loved, like them, to meditate in the early morning, to offer worship with flowers and kum-kum in the temple, and to spend the day in service, loving God and offering Him her heart with every thought. Who, she wondered, could ever wish for more than this?

Her brother, Nivritti, was the quiet one. He felt still such a strong bond of love for his Guru, Gahini, that he thought almost continually of him, sensing his presence with him at all times. He reflected often on the teachings he had received at the feet of his master, and often reminisced on their many private moments together in the hidden cave. He lived for nothing else but his periods of deep meditation, and the divine experiences which came to him unbidden at those times. He felt no attraction at all to the world, and regarded it with supreme detachment. The extraordinary peace and joy which he derived from his prolonged periods of meditation far outweighed any delight he had ever found through the senses. His inner joy was so full that no amount of occurrances in the outer world could either add to or detract from it. The parade of the world he viewed as a magic lantern show of ephemeral forms which appeared and disappeared as mere images upon the cosmic screen, while he, the eternal witness, ever blissful, remained ever unchanged.

In this respect, Jnaneshvar was much like Nivritti; so absorbed was he in his inner joy that he could sit for hours and hours, just watching the play of thoughts, images and revelations, or engrossed in intense concentration on the ever-facinating light that hovered just inside his forehead, and which revealed to him so many hidden wonders and delights. Indeed, it seems that it was at this wonderfully peaceful time in his life that Jnaneshvar realized his identity with the universal Self.

Of course, there is no record of the date and circumstances of Jnaneshvar's enlightenment, but the evidence would seem to indicate that it occurred around this period, from 1287 to 1288, at Nevasa. The *Jnaneshvari*, which he wrote in 1290, at the age of nineteen, is sufficient evidence to the wise that Jnandev had fully realized the Self some time prior to its writing. He had also obtained considerable learning to substantiate his own experience in the meanwhile, and was able in *Jnaneshvari* to speak with the utmost confidence of the knowledge of the Self, both from his own first-hand experience and from the recorded experiences of his predecessors. Therefore, it is safe to assume that at least a few years had elapsed between his own realization and the writing of *Jnaneshvari*.

It is also apparent that, from Jnaneshvar's perspective, such experience came to him by the grace of his Guru and beloved brother, Nivritti. We must assume, then, that Nivritti himself had attained *samadhi* previous to Jnaneshvar's attainment, and had closely supervised his younger brother's *sadhana*, encouraging him, and deeply influencing, by his own example, Jnaneshvar's profound longing for God-knowledge. Perhaps it happened something like this:

In the early morning, long before dawn, Nivritti and Jnandev had bathed silently in the moonlit river, and had taken their accustomed seats on the river bank. Both boys were so inwardly concentrated that no word was spoken, yet both sensed the extraordinary condition of stillness and intense clarity which seemed to pervade not only their own consciousness, but the whole universe. Jnaneshvar's attention was entirely centered on the spreading white light which he could see and feel gathering at the crown of his head. With his eyelids lightly closed, and his gaze fixed on that clear, cooling light, his breath became soft and gentle, nearly suspended in the pure silence and calm of his uplifted awareness.

O what a pure and perfect state! What loving sweetness filled his mind and body! He felt balanced, poised, on the threshold of absolute purity and clarity of mind, and he looked to the infinite heights of light and silence above with all the desperate longing of his being. "O loving Father, lift me up to Thyself so that I may know Thee and proclaim Thee to all Thy children!" It was a prayer that spoke itself from his soul to the impenetrable light into which he peered. And suddenly, as he leaned with all his concentration into that utter stillness, his mind grew bright with clarity, and he knew.

"I have been blinded by my own feeling of individuality! I have been like a pebble yearning for the stone of which it is made. Or like a wave yearning for the ocean. There is only one Being, one Existence; I and God are not two, but always the One. I am always the only Life, the only one, who exists as everything. How had I imagined I was separate, apart? Like a man who dreams he is fallen in a ditch, and dreams a cast of thousands to inhabit his dream along with him, I have dreamt I was a player among others in my own drama. I am the Dreamer and the dream. All this is myself, and nothing is outside of me ever. I am this gossamer universe of worlds upon worlds, drama upon drama. All is me! Yet all is but a bubble of my own fantasy; I remain forever pure and free, unmanifest and unseen, silently upholding in myself this vast array of form and life. There is no other, but only Me; it is my Life which sings and dances in a million million forms, forever untouched and unchanged."

Clearly, he saw the myriad universe emerging from and returning to himself, as a breath passes out and is then indrawn again. All was known, all was himself, and he was exquisitely, happily, alone.

When, at last, he raised his eyelids, the daylight had long since come; and here he was, once again, amid the world of forms. But nothing had changed; it was all himself, only now he was seeing from the vantage-point of one of the forms within his own play. He could see the river flowing by, a sparkling sheet of consciousness; the monastery grounds were, likewise, consciousness, every glistening speck of sand. And there, looking at him, with such love and beauty, was Nivritti, his own Self in the form of brother, guide and benefactor.

Nivritti had been sitting there for some while, watching his brother's face, and he knew that young Jnandev had reached that supreme knowledge which he also had known. Their eyes showered rays of love on one another, as they sat smiling deleriously at the living form of God before them. Jnandev's vision was clouded with tears of joy and gratitude as he delighted in the shimmering form of Nivritti before him. Then he prostrated himself fully on the ground before his brother, and saluted him with "Om namo Narayanaya. Jaya Gurudev! Jaya Gurudev!"

8 THE CREATIONS OF THE POET

What unbounded happiness Jnaneshvar experienced in the following weeks and months! He walked about in an enchanted world, a smile gently playing on his face at all times. All could see the radiant aura which surrounded him, and everyone remarked at the exquisite beauty of his countenance. Naturally, Jnandev spoke of nothing else but God; he had come to know the very truth of existence, and he spoke of it to all who cared to listen. Also, he took a renewed interest in the writings and declarations of the sages before him who had known the Self. He spent many hours reading and re-reading the words of the great illumined rishis of India's glorious past.

He had found an abundant source of pleasure in the library of books which Satchidananda possessed in the monastery. His favorites were the *Srimad Bhagavata Purana*, whose stories of the youth of Krishna still made him thrill with divine emotion, and the *Bhagavad Gita*, which never ceased to amaze him with its clear instructive wisdom.

One night, after their evening meal, everyone was relaxing, when Jnandev brought out the *Gita* and opened it to the beginning chapter. The Swami, who was sitting nearby, noticed, and said, "As long as you're beginning it again, and we're all sitting here, why don't you read it aloud to us, and explain as you go along."

Jnandev laughed; "I'll read it," he asid, "but I don't think I could explain what Krishna says any better than he does himself."

"Oh, come on," said Muktabai; "you know you can explain it better than anyone. Do, please. We'll all be very still and listen."

"Who wants to hear Jnani comment on the Gita?" prompted the Swami.

Everyone shouted, "Yes!" loudly, and so Jnaneshvar surrendered and began. First he read out the passage from the Gita, and then, in his own enthusiastic and delightful way, he elaborated on Krishna's words, elucidating his meaning with great skill and clarity. Every night he read a chapter, and at the end of eighteen nights he had completed the entire Gita, and completely enthralled his listeners, clarifying some aspects of

Krishna's teachings which even the Swami had not previously understood.

"Jnaneshvar," said Satchidananda, after the last of the commentaries. "I think you should write down this commentary of yours for the benefit of everyone. It is really extraordinary; there is nothing like it in our language!"

"Let some great scholar write a commentary," said Jnaneshvar; "who am I to write a commentary?"

But Nivritti sided with the Swami, saying, "Brother, you have a rare gift for revealing the hidden truths of the Gita to make it come alive. It is God's gift, and it would be a service to all Maharashtrans if you would put your commentary in a written form."

Jnaneshvar remained silent for a moment; then he said, "Nivritti, since you request it, I shall do as you wish. You are my Gurudev, and with your blessings, I shall undertake to accomplish this work."

The Swami beamed with pleasure; "If you like," he offered, "I will serve as your scribe, and while you dictate it, I will take it all down."

Nivritti too seemed pleased; "You see, the Lord has provided you with everything. You will make a very good book."

II

On the following morning, Satchidananda gathered up the ink, quills and stack of palm-leaf *talas* he had prepared the night before, and carried them outside into the warm morning air. Jnandev was already seated in the *Panchavati*, the little grove of five trees where the holy recitals were held. Nivritti was also there, sitting erectly in the *padmasana* position. Both had been there, meditating, since several hours before the first light, and now they were sitting, relaxed and slightly tipsy, with a glow of happy delight on their faces.

Satchidananda arranged himself comfortably in a cross-legged sitting position and spread his *talas*, quills and ink-pot about him in his systematic way. At last he sat upright and signalled to the amused faces of Jnandev and Nivritti that he was prepared to begin. Jnandev and Nivritti closed their eyes. Satchidananda also closed his. For a moment they all sat there in the sweet silence of the morning, broken only by the gurgling of the river a few feet away. Then, from

Jnandev came the rich deep sound of:

Om-m-m Shree Ganeshaya namah
Shree Parabrahma namah
Jayatmavidya shuddha swayarupam

Satchidananda began to write, hurriedly taking down Jnandev's words. Jnaneshvar praised the various scriptures and their authors, comparing each one to some sensual delight, and praised the six systems of philosophy as adornments to the figure of Ganesha, the god of blessings, the remover of obstacles. Then, after saluting Sharada, the goddess of speech and learning, he offered his salutations to Nivritti as his Guru, to whose grace he attributed all his good fortune.

Having done all that, he began to extol Vyasa, the author of the *Mahabharata*, in which the *Bhagavad Gita* is contained, comparing him to the Sun by whose light the whole world is illumined. And the *Mahabharata* itself he compared to a lotus of which the *Gita* is the pollen. This pollen, he said, carrying his analogy a bit further, can be carried away by the bee of the mind which ponders its deep meaning. Then, addressing his imaginary audience of sages, he beseeched them all to listen to his story.

With great respect, he humbled himself before his invisible listeners, protesting that, though he was but a child and ignorant, still he was granted some understanding of the Gita through the grace of his Guru, Nirvritti; and that therefore they should hear him out. "Please add whatever may be found lacking," he said, "and reject whatever may be superfluous." And then, turning to Nivritti, who was beginning to look impatient with this long preamble, he said, "What you inspire in me I will speak, just as a puppet dances according to the strings that are pulled by the puppeteer. I am obedient to your grace and the grace of the saints; therefore make of me whatever you wish."

At this, Nivritti, finally giving in to his impatience, blurted out, "Enough! You don't need to say all of this!" And, patting his copy of the Gita, he said, "Now give your mind to this work!" And Jnandev, smiling at his brother's predictable response to his own weakness for rambling embellishment, put aside for the moment his poetic flight, and began the story of the dialogue between Krishna and Arjuna on the battlefield of Kurukshetra.

III

All through the hot summer months, Jnaneshvar gave his mind wholly to the writing of his commentaries on the Gita. In the afternoons he would go over with Satchidananda the writings of that morning, and in the evenings, he would contemplate the upcoming verses and would compose in his mind what he was going to say on the morrow. It was a time of immense happiness for Jnandev, for he felt as though he was an instrument of divine wisdom through which great beauty and knowledge were being given to the world. At the same time, immersed so deeply as he was in the profound thoughts of the Gita, the very words of Krishna, he was transformed as a chameleon is transformed by its background, and he became wholly transparent to the divine light which illumined his mind.

He became that light and that knowledge; day and night he lived in an intensely focused height of awareness, scarcely conscious of his own separate existence. He knew with absolute certainty that it was God's own intelligence which was filling him, inspiring him to know and to speak such utterly magnificent words of beauty and truth, and he offered his soul prostrate every moment at that divine fountainhead in a continual prayer to remain in His grace, and in such glorious service.

Jnaneshvar was entirely consumed in his dedication to the completion of his work on the Gita, and all of his beloved companions knew also that something very extraordinary and wonderful was being created; and they did what they could to serve in the process of its completion as well. Satchidananda was overjoyed to be a part of so miraculous a work; he soared in happiness as he copied out at night the words he had hastily inscribed on his palm-leaves that morning. And each new morning he thrilled with excitement to hear each new addition to thc growing manuscript. As he listened and wrote, he was filled anew with awe and admiration for this young man, and he sang in his heart, "Praise God! Praise God!"

When, at last, they had reached the last part of the eighteenth chapter, eveyone was aware that a divine miracle was occurring in their midst. For Jnaneshvar's

Bhavartadipika (later to be known simply as *Jnaneshvari*) was no ordinary book. It was a work of unearthly beauty and angelic purity; cast in the Marathi language, in the Ovi metre, it was like nothing that had ever been seen before. It was entirely unique among books, having no peer anywhere. It represented the highest wisdom of which mortal man is capable, framed in the sweetest language by the purest heart that ever lived -- their own brother, their own dear, amazing Jnandev.

IV

By the time of the rainy season, in the year 1290, *Jnaneshvari* was completed, and bound with cords in several volumes. It was finally done; it was a permanent treasure to be shared with all posterity. But, as is usually the case after a prolonged creative effort, its author felt utterly drained and disquieted -- even depressed. Weeks passed, and his mood became one of dissatisfaction and restlessness. He began to write out his thoughts, thoughts which had been stirred from the bottom of his mind by the focus upon the issues discussed in the Gita. The Gita, for all its exquisite beauty and profound depths, was an expression of the eternal truth, which, like any such expression, was limited by its historical and cultural setting in time. There were parts of it which, to Jnandev, were archaic; for example, the division of men into godly and demonic and the general emphasis on the dualistic perspective of Sankhya philosophy, which he was obliged to support with commentary. Thus, he felt that he had been somewhat constrained in his freedom of expression by the obligation to follow a form and conception not his own; and now he longed to speak freely, in his own way, to address some of the philosophical issues which were so misunderstood and misrepresented in his own times.

Nivritti had taught him the Shaivite philosophical terminology adopted by the Natha sect to which Gahininath belonged. And he himself had read many philosophical works not only of the ancients but of some modern commentators as well, such as Mukundaraj and some of the Mahanubhavas. Now he felt drawn to address some of these contemporary issues, and he spoke often with Nivritti of his thoughts and feelings in regard to the doctrines of some of the more popular sects active in Maharashtra.

Nivritti saw that Jnandev was bursting still with creative energy and desired to speak his mind fully, and so one day he said to Jnaneshvar, "Look, your *Bhavartadipika* is finished; but you have more to say. I wish you would write an independent work, following your own guidelines, and expressing your own philosophical understanding." Jnaneshvar was delighted. Immediately fired with enthusiasm, nearly exploding with thoughts, he began the composition -- alone this time -- of his own book of mystical knowledge. He had adopted the terminology of the Vaishnavas in his treatment of the *Bhagavad Gita*, using the name of Vishnu and of Krishna who was his incarnation to represent the Absolute, the Godhead; this time, he would adopt the terminology of the Shaivites, and use the name of Shiva to represent the Godhead.

In *Jnaneshvari*, he had conformed to the terminology of Vyasa, and had utilized the ancient Sankhya terms, *Purusha* and *Prakrti* to speak of the apparent division between the transcendent and the immanent aspects of the one Reality. But Vyasa wrote long before Shankara had come to revitalize the Vedanta philosophy, and long before Buddhism had flooded and then retreated from the land of Bharata. Much philosophical haranguing and confusion had been promulgated in the interim, and it was to the dispelling of that confusion that Jnandev now addressed himself.

This time, it was Jnaneshvar alone who sat in the Panchavati in the early morning, writing upon his palm leaves, deep in thought. It was the apparent duality of *Purusha* and *Prakrti* which once again occupied his mind, but this time he spoke of them as *Shiva* and *Shakti*. Conceiving of these two aspects of the One as divine lovers, he portrayed them in his poetic imagination as inseparable components of Reality, as inseparable as musk and its fragrance, or as fire and its heat:

When He embraces Her,
It is His own bliss that Shiva enjoys.
He is the Enjoyer of everything,
But there is no enjoyment without Her.
She is His form,
But Her beauty comes from Him.
By their intermingling,
They are together enjoying this feast.

It was in this way Jnandev began his *Amritanubhav*; with a brilliant poetic metaphor, he portrayed the two abstract principles, Shiva and Shakti, as an ephemeral couple whose duality disappears when they embrace, just as the opposites of day and night both disappear at the breaking of dawn:

> If night and day were to approach the Sun,
> Both would disappear.
> In the same way, the duality of Shiva and Shakti
> Would disappear if their essential Unity were seen.

Thus he acknowledged the existence of the apparent duality between the world and God, between subject and object, yet revealed the essential Unity from which these opposites are born -- a Unity which is experienced by man only when his mind becomes wholly merged in God.

What Jnaneshvar wrote in 1290-91, at the age of twenty, that book which came to be known as *Amritanubhav*, "The Nectar Of Mystical Experience", is, arguably, the greatest masterpiece of mystical philosophy ever written. It remains as a timeless reassurance to all who long for Truth that, through love, God can be experienced and known as one's own innermost Self.

9 A NEW SULTAN COMES TO POWER

In 1287, the same year that saw the death of Rakhu and the pilgrimage of Jnaneshvar and his family, the reign of Balban, the great Sultan of Delhi, came to an end with his death; and the Muslim populace there was viewing with much apprehension the ascendency of their new ruler. With Balban dead, his grandson, Muiz-ud-din Kaikubad, a handsome nineteen-year old youth, was proclaimed the new Sultan and Emperor of India. But Muiz-ud-din, who had been constrained to a life of sensual deprivation under his austere grandfather, now gave free rein to his appetites, and turned every day in the palace into a gay orgy of drunken revelry. The historian, Barani, describes Kaikubad's reign in extravagant prose:

> Voluptuaries and convivialists, seekers of pleasure, purveyors of wit, and inventors of buffooneries, who had been kept in the background, lurking, unemployed, without a customer for their wares, now came into demand. Courtesans appeared in the shadow of every wall, and elegant forms sunned themselves on every balcony. Not a street but sent forth a master of melody, or a chanter of odes. In every quarter a singer or a song-writer lifted up his head ... So the emperor, Mu'iz-ud-din, and the nobles of his realm and empire, and the children of the peers and princes of his time, and the gay, the rich, the sensualists and the epicures who lived under his rule, one and all gave themselves up to gluttony and idleness and pleasure and merriment, and the heart of high and low alike were engaged in wine and love and song and carnival... [13]

Poor Kaikubad became so ill from his uncustomary debaucheries that he soon became unfit to keep up even a semblance of rulership; and in 1289, his three-year old son was formally proclaimed Sultan in his stead.

Meanwhile, a certain officer of the court, Malik Yaghrash Firuz, leader of a large influential clan known as the Khalji, who had recently been appointed by Kaikubad as Minister of the Army, suddenly found himself under attack by some of the other court nobles who, thinking to stem his power, spread abroad the rumor that the Khaljis were not of pure Turkish stock. The Khaljis, though longtime residents of Afghanistan who had migrated to India several generations back, were, in fact, of Turkish descent; but Firuz's opponents were bent on preventing the Khaljis from obtaining any further influence, and were plotting to murder Firuz. Learning of this plot, Firuz gathered together his clansmen and supporters and turned the tables on his enemies. With the army at his command, he made a surprise raid on the palace, and carried away the three year-old Emperor, and sent his men to dispatch the sickly Kaikubad. According to the historian, Ferishta, they found Kaikubad in his bedroom, "lying on his bed in a dying state... They beat out his brains with bludgeons, and then, rolling him up in his bed-clothes, threw him out of the window into the river." [14]

After some time, when he had established his power over all the government forces, Firuz had the infant Emperor murdered as well, and on June 13, 1290, he proclaimed himself Sultan Jalal-uddin Firuz Khalji.

Thus, the revolution of the Khaljis put an end to the previous reign of the Ilbari Turks. And, though the new Sultan, Jalal-uddin, appointed many of his own relations to the most valued positions in the government, he kept on many of the old guard as well. Malik Chhajju, for example, who was nephew to Balban and the only survivor of the late royal family, was allowed to retain the fiefdom of the substantially large province of Kera; but Jalal-uddin's own younger brother, ennobled as Yaghrush Khan, was appointed Minister of the Army, his nephews, Ala-uddin and Almas Beg, received important posts, and his three sons were given the titles of Khan Khanan, Arkali Khan, and Kadr Khan.

Sultan Jalal-uddin was not a young man; he was already seventy years old when he ascended the throne at Delhi. As a lifelong soldier, by now he had become tired of killing, and had become extremely lenient and good-natured even toward his avowed enemies. In fact, because of his unduly generous attitude toward those who outrightly opposed him, some of the people close to him thought him a bit feeble-minded and incapable of providing the strength required of a ruler. One example of the Sultan's leniency occurred when Malik Chhajju, the previously mentioned nephew of Balban, decided to make his bid for the throne and declared his province of Kera an independent state. Gathering together some of the old Balbanite nobles, he marched on Delhi with a large force of men. But he was defeated just outside the city at Badaun by the forces of the Sultan, led by his nephew, Ala-uddin.

When Malik Chhajju and his lieutenants were brought before the Sultan, Jalal-uddin not only released them, but entertained them and commended them on their loyalty to their former ruler. However, he did take away from Chhajju the fiefdom of Kera, bestowing it on his twenty-two year old nephew, Ala-uddin, who had played so great a part in subduing the rebels. There was at least one occasion, however, when the Sultan's proverbial leniency did not come to the offender's rescue. It was in the sad but noteworthy case of Sayiddi Maula.

Sayiddi Maula was a Moslem holy man who instituted in Delhi an Academy and hospice for travellers, fakirs, and the poor of all denominations. It is said that he turned no one away from his door. He kept no women, nor slaves, and lived upon rice alone. But he spent so much money in charity on feeding and clothing the poor, that everyone believed him to possess miraculous powers. He gave huge quantities of gold to the needy, pointing out rocks under which the treasure could be found; he threw magnificent feasts welcoming everyone in the city. Ferishta, the historian, records that he expended daily on the poor, "about 1000 maunds of flour, 500 maunds of meat, 200 maunds of sugar, along with rice, oil, butter, and other necessities in proportion." [15]

One day, a man came to the Sultan, saying that he had overheard Sayiddi Maula plotting to assasinate the Sultan; and so Sayiddi Maula was ordered brought to the court under arrest. As he protested innocence, and no other witness appeared against him, the Sultan ordered that he should stand the ordeal by fire to prove his innocence. But just at the moment that Sayiddi Maula, after saying his prayers, was about to walk through the fire, the Sultan, being advised by his counsellors, decided that this was not a just trial, as the fire pays no more respect to the innocent than to the guilty. So he sentenced Sayiddi Maula to be held in a dungeon beneath the palace. However, while they were taking Sayiddi Maula through the streets, the Sultan shouted from his balcony to some of his supporters, "Behold the man who was projecting such evil against us. I leave him to be judged by you, according to his deserts." With this, one man, a religious fanatic, ran forward and began slashing Sayiddi Maula with a razor.

Sayiddi Maula offered no resistance, but only asked the man to send him to God immediately. Then he looked up to the balcony where Jalal-uddin stood, and addressed him, saying, "I am rejoiced that you have thought to put an end to my life, yet it is sinful to distress the pious and the innocent; be assured that my curse will lie heavy upon you and your unfortunate posterity!" At this, the Sultan's son, Arkali Khan, who hated Sayiddi Maula, and who may have been behind the plot to implicate him in treason, beckoned to a mahout, who was ready mounted atop a large elephant, to advance and trample Sayiddi Maula to death.

Zia-uddin Barani, who witnessed the carrying out of this order, reports that immediately after the death of Sayiddi Maula, a black whirlwind arose, which, for the space of half an hour, changed day into night, and drove the people in the streets against one another, so that they could scarcely find their ways home. He went on to say that, during that entire year, A.D. 1291, no rain fell in those provinces, and a famine ensued, killing thousands of citizens who died daily in the streets and highways, while whole families drowned themselves in the river. The Sultan's eldest son, Khan Khanan, died, falling victim to the pestilence which followed.

II

Shortly after this incident, Jalal-uddin led an expedition to Ranthambhor, but when the Rana of Ranthambhor shut himself and his army inside the fort, the Sultan decided not to besiege it, saying that he did not consider ten such forts worth a single hair of a Muslim's head; and he returned to Delhi on June 3, 1291. In the year 1292, Hulagu Khan, grandson of Ghengis Khan, invaded northern India with over 100,000 troops, and Jalal-uddin, at the head of his army, went forward to meet them. After a great battle, Jalal-uddin defeated the Mongols, and took about a thousand prisoners; he did not pursue his victory, however, but instead offered peace to the Mongols, and safe passage. The invaders gladly accepted Jalal-uddin's offer, and several thousand of them consented to become Muslims in order to remain as citizens of Delhi. Jalal-uddin sealed this pact by giving one of his daughters in marriage to Hulagu Khan, and a happy peace was thereby affected.

Meanwhile, around this same time, Ala-uddin, the Sultan's nephew, at his estate in Kera, had been lavishly entertaining a group of disaffected nobles who had been the supporters of the ill-fated Malik Chhajju. It was to Ala-uddin that they were now offering their support. It would be a simple matter, they assured him, to take the throne from his dim-witted uncle, if only he could somehow amass sufficient funds to hire and outfit an army. That, they said, had been the deficiency in Malik Chhajju's coup attempt; he hadn't had enough money to support a sufficiently large army. Ala-uddin thought about this, and he saw that he would have to build up a force gradually, so that one day, one day ...

One day, in the year 1294, Ala-uddin went to his uncle at court and suggested that he take a small force of men and attack the city of Bhilsa which lay just south of his own governorship of Kera, and where there had recently been some rebellious uprisings. The Sultan readily approved, for he was very proud of and lovingly disposed toward his brave and charming nephew. And so, shortly thereafter, Ala-uddin set out at the head of his own army toward the unguarded town of Bhilsa. It was an easy victory. Ala-uddin sacked the city, and destroyed the temples, taking a pair of large brass idols to be carried back with him to Delhi and buried at the Badaun gates so they might be trod upon by the faithful of Islam, as was the custom.

It was while there at Bhilsa that one of Ala-uddin's generals remarked to him that it was a pity that it was not Devgiri they were taking, for the treasure accumulated there was beyond any man's dreams. Ala-uddin looked south, toward the Vindhya mountain slopes beyond which lay the kingdom of Devgiri, and at that moment a plan was hatched in his mind.

When Ala-uddin returned to Delhi with his booty, and turned over most of it to his uncle, Jalal-uddin was very pleased with his fine young nephew, and, as a reward, conferred on him the governorship of Oudh, in addition to his present governorship of Kera. Ala-uddin, playing the worshipful nephew, lovingly expressed his gratitude, and then proposed that when the revenues from Kera and Oudh were collected at the end of the year, he be allowed to use them for the outfitting of a small army for the purpose of conquering yet another rich city, the city of Chandheri, just to the southwest of Kera.

Again pleased with the zeal of his apparently dutiful and conscientious nephew, Jalal-uddin readily assented. How fortunate, he thought to himself, to have a real warrior in the family, to fill the coffers of the Sultanate and to defend the holy religion of the Prophet. Later, when his wife, Mullika Jehan, warned the Sultan to be wary of so ambitious a young prince, Jalal-uddin only laughed. "Don't be ridiculous!" he chided; "I raised that boy, and he loves me like a father. His only wish is to serve the Empire and to make his old uncle proud of him. How suspicious you are, woman! The boy is the son of my brother; I trust him with my life!" Mullika Jehan only sighed, knowing it was useless to protest any further.

III

As Ala-uddin returned from Delhi to Kera on horseback with his entourage, his general, Nusrat Khan, rode closely alongside him. "So," said Nasrut Khan, happily, "he agreed to an invasion of Chandheri! When do we go?"

"Not till February -- when the hot season begins," answered Ala-uddin.

"Why wait so long? It's only a short journey! We could be back before our fires have died out."

"But we're not going to Chandheri," said Ala-uddin.

"But you said ..."

Ala-uddin smiled at the bewilderment of his general; "We will appear to be going to Chandheri," said Ala-uddin, "but we will turn due south and head into the mountains before we reach Chandheri."

For a moment, Nasrut Khan looked puzzled; then his eyes widened, and he exclaimed, "Devgiri!"

"Shhh ...," whispered Ala-uddin, looking around to see who might have heard.

"By the beard of Allah!" Nasrut Khan whispered this time. And then he laughed aloud, excited and delighted by the thought of taking the resplendent city of gold, the fabled kingdom of the Yadavas -- Devgiri, 'the mountain of God'.

IV

The great fortressed city of Devgiri lay several hundred miles to the south, on the other side of the rugged Vindhya mountains, and through treacherous jungles; moreover, it was unreachable except through unfriendly Hindu kingdoms who might, themselves, give battle, or warn of any approach to Devgiri. The walled city of Devgiri itself sat upon the top of a massive cone-shaped hill 640 feet high, accessible by only one passageway which could be effectively sealed. All around it stretched the vast plains of the Deccan as far as one could see.

Never had the kingdom of Devgiri been invaded by a foreign enemy. It was regarded by everyone as impregnable. On its northern border stood the mountain range; to the south, the powerful Hoysala kingdom with its capital at Dwarasamudra; to the east, the Ganapati armies at Telingana in Rajmundri; and to the west, the Western Ghats. Thus, Devgiri was isolated and protected from all foreign infiltration by great powerful kingdoms and natural barriers which surrounded it. Since the 10th century, the Muslim invaders had poured into India from the north, and never had they presented a threat to Devgiri; but this was the end of the 13th century, and the wolfish Ala-uddin was hungry for conquest.

It is highly unlikely that Jnaneshvar and his family, who had been living happily at Nevasa for most of this time, relatively isolated from the concerns of the world, were even aware of the death of Balban and the chain of events which followed upon it in far-off Delhi. They were entirely engrossed in their spiritual studies and practices and in their service to God, without the slightest inkling of the effect that events in Delhi would soon have on their destiny.

10 THE PILGRIMS OF PANDHARPUR

In the year 1293, Swami Satchidananda died peacefully in his sleep. "His heart just stopped," the doctor from the village said. And the youngsters, as one, realized that their stay at Nevasa had come to an end.

"In Pandharpur, God's name is sung day and night to the sound of music," said Jnaneshvar one evening as they all sat at their meal. Nivritti kept eating silently with his head bowed as usual. Sopan looked quickly from one to another and glanced at Muktabai. Muktabai was trying not to smile, but she could not conceal it. Everyone knew after that that they were going to Pandharpur.

They had been at the quiet little monastery in Nevasa for six wonderful years. And now they were off on a new adventure -- to Pandharpur, the city of God, a city of towering temples, where the sound of *kirtana* and dancing filled the streets, where Panduranga himself stood gleaming and giving his blessing to the children of the city. Pandharpur! The sound of the name sang in Muktabai's heart, and she was so filled with excitement and fabulous dreams that she could scarcely bear it. "When will we go?" she whispered softly to Jnandev.

"Soon," he said.

Muktabai clung to his arm and squeezed it with excitement. "But when?" she urged.

"We must inform the officials in the town that we are leaving; then we will go."

"Oh! I will have to start packing everything! Oh!" And Muktabai began to laugh as she hugged her brother and swung him around in her embrace.

Within two days they were ready to go. Early in the morning they gathered in the Panchavati to meditate and to thank the Lord for their beautiful home for the past six years, and to request his blessing on their journey. They laid flowers on the grave of Satchidananda, and on his sandals which were left on the altar in the Panchavati. Then Jnandev hugged the great peepul tree under which he had sat to write his *Bhavarthadipika* and his *Amritanubhav*. He touched his head to the ground, and took one more look at the place where he had so often communed in the early morning with his Lord; and then he joined the others on the road in front of the monastery. With one final salute to their lovely monastery, they set off -- three young men, a girl of nineteen, and a donkey, which had been the parting gift of the citizens of Nevasa, laden high with food, clothing and utensils -- on the road to Pandharpur.

II

The records are very scant concerning the next few years of the life of Jnaneshvar and his family, but it appears they all went first to Alandi, where they spent a few joyful days with their maternal grandparents and other relatives, and then travelled on together southeast, along the banks of the Bhima river, toward the enchanting and holy city of Pandharpur.

How Pandharpur came to be a holy city to which thousands of pilgrims travelled each year had been told to Jnaneshvar and his siblings by their father long ago. According to the legend, a young man by the name of Pundalik lived there at one time who was extraordinarily dedicated to the service of God in the form of his parents. All day long, he worked to care for their every need. One day -- so the story goes --, while he was scrubbing the floors of his parents' home, Krishna, having heard of Pundalik's single-minded devotion, came in person to pay him a visit. Pundalik, however, was so totally absorbed in his work, scrubbing the floor, that he had no time for visitors. And so, tossing a brick to Krishna, he told him to stand on that while he scrubbed around him. Krishna obligingly stood on the brick, and was so impressed by the single-minded dedication of Pundalik that he caused his own form to become solidified in this pose as a statue, thus making a present of his own form to Pundalik. No one knew whether this story was true or not, but at least it offered an explanation of why the *murti* of Krishna in the temple of Pandharpur was standing on a brick with his hands on his hips.

Over the years many miracles were attributed to this statue, and it câme to be regarded by many devotees as the actual form of Krishna. *Kirtana* (devotional singing) was performed to it day and night, and each year a gala festival was held by the Pandharpur devotees (*Varkaris*), in which the form of Krishna was carried through the streets of the city to the sound of cymbals and mridungs, and the singing of:

Vitthale! Vitthale!
Vitthale! Vitthale!
Jaya Jaya Vitthale!
Jaya Jaya Vitthale!

Krishna had so many names, no one knew them all; but in Pandharpur he was known only by a few special names: he was called Vitthale (*Veet-ha-lay*) or Vitthala, or Panduranga, or Vithoba.

Jnaneshvar walked happily along the road with his brothers and sister, thinking of how he would soon be seeing Panduranga at last. He had eaten well at Alandi and had rested well, and he felt very strong and exhuberant as he walked along in the dawning sunshine toward Pandharpur. A song began in his heart, and he gave voice to it in the clear morning air:

Rama Krishna Hare
Mukunda Murare
Rama Krishna Hare
Mukunda Murare
Panduranga! Panduranga!
Panduranga! Panduranga!
Panduranga Hare
Panduranga Hare

The others took up the chant, and they sang it nearly all the way to Pandharpur.

At last Jnandev and his family had arrived at the outskirts of the holy city. It was nearly dusk of the third day of their journey, and they were all tired and hungry as they made their way into the city; but they knew they had to go to the temple first to kneel before Vitthala and offer thanks for their safe arrival. The temple was the largest and most beautiful any of them had ever seen. It was surrounded with a porch of marble with marble steps, and reached into the sky like a huge juggernaut. At the entrance were beautiful statues, also made of marble, of the heavenly guards holding crossed maces.

As they entered, they caught sight of Vithoba right away. Black as pitch, with a gold embroidered red silk shawl draped around its shoulders and garlands of fragrant flowers about its neck, it stood, shining, at the front of the temple. Two priests sat nearby behind a low silver railing, and a few pilgrims were prostrating before the *murti*.

Each of the children approached the statue in turn; Jnandev approached it, following Mukti, his eyes wide in admiration for the supernatural splendor of the glorious Vithoba who shone with a living light. Prostrating fully on the floor, he offered his heart to the Lord, and felt himself swallowed in a blinding, all-embracing, luminous bliss, which moved up his spine and poured like liquid golden nectar into his ecstatic brain. For a moment, Jnaneshvar lost all recollection of where he was. Then, becoming aware of the impropriety of remaining there on the floor, he rose and made his way to the rear of the temple where he sat with his back against the marble wall.

The tears flowed from the outer corners of his eyes and down his cheeks uncontrollably. He felt as though the Lord were carressing him, and with each stroke of His hand raising a thrill that moved upward along his spine only to burst in a shower of almost unbearable joy within his brain. "O Hari, Hari, Hari," he repeated in his mind. He opened his eyes and looked at the dark statue facing him from the other end of the temple. It seemed to be smiling at him, and in its posture, with hands on hips, seemed to be saying, "Well, what did you expect!"

Jnaneshvar closed his eyes and once again returned to the inner effulgence that seemed to be emanating from the top of his head. As he focused on this light, his tiredness dissolved, and his mind became extraordinarily alert and clear and still. The veil of separate identity lifted, and all at once, there was no more Jnaneshvar, no more temple, no more Lord of Jnaneshvar; no more anything but the one intensely awake Being who quietly experienced himself as everything.

When he opened his eyes again, Mukti and Nivritti and Sopan were kneeling beside him, and Mukti was applying a cold towel to his head. Soon they were all laughing, as they were off to find some temporary shelter, and to prepare a meal after their long journey.

For the next few days, Jnaneshvar stayed close to the

temple. During the day, he sat in his usual spot against the wall, and wrote songs to God. One of the *abhangas* he wrote at this time, began:

> O Panduranga, I came to see you,
> But when we met, you disappeared.
> Yet, more amazing than that,
> You made me disappear as well.
> Now, I ask you, O Hari,
> Where is the seer and where is the seen?

In the evenings, the people of Pandharpur gathered in the temple for *arati*, the waving of a tray of lights in worship of the *murti*; and later, many came to sing *kirtana*. There were mridungs and tabla and vinas, and hand cymbals; and the music would begin with a slow, plaintive melody:

> *Narayana, Narayana*
> *Jaya Govinda Hare*
> *Narayana, Narayana*
> *Jaya Gopala Hare*

After some time, the beat would quicken to a driving, pulsating rhythm, and the bodies of the women would begin to sway. Then, gradually, the music would increase in volume and intensity, along with the beat, to become a rising, swelling, tide of call and response, reaching to a final shattering crescendo of sound and joy.

Jnandev had never experienced anything so wonderful in his life. 'It's true,' he thought; 'this is the heavenly city of joy.' After the *kirtana*, he'd sit once again in his place against the wall, and pray to Hari to lift him into the pure free sky of Unity once again. The *kirtana* drew his heart and mind to such heights of longing combined with joy ... and yet when he sat to meditate, he found himself drawn into an utter stillness and peace so profound, he seemed to float in a calm blue ocean of light and silent joy.

Jnandev felt he could remain in Pandharpur forever. He felt such tender and overwhelming love for the people of this city, though he knew no one at all. They were all angels, of that he was sure. And he would be happy to remain forever listening to their heavenly voices singing the name of God. There were a number of young men, around his own age, who came regularly to the temple for the *kirtana*, some of whom often remained behind, like himself, to sit for a long while at the rear of the temple.

One morning, when he went to bathe in the river, he saw there one of the young men whom he had often seen at the temple. The young man saluted him and Jnandev offered his *namaskar* in return. Later in the morning, after his meditation, when he saw the young man coming out of the temple, he decided to speak to him; but before he could speak, the young man said, "Hello, friend. Where do you come from?"

Jnaneshvar told him, and asked him if he lived permanently at Pandharpur. "Yes," he said, "but I've only been here for a few months; I came from near Devgiri."

"My name is Jnandev," said Jnaneshvar.

"And I am Namadev, said the young man. Instantly, the two were fast friends. They both loved God, and loved to sing His name; and that was enough. Jnaneshvar now had a friend with whom he could talk and from whom he could learn the *kirtana* of Pandharpur. Namadev showed him about the city and told him the history of every stone.

"Tell me about yourself," Jnandev said to Namadev one day. "I have told you all about my life, my brothers and sister, and now you know everything about me. Now you must tell me something about yourself."

"Well," said Namadev, "before I came to Pandharpur, I was a bandit, a *dacoit*."

"Come on," said Jnandev, laughing; "tell me the truth."

"I am telling you the truth,"Namadev insisted. "I was born at the village of Narasi Vamani, just outside Devgiri, on October 26, 1270. My father is Damaset, a tailor, and my mother is Gonabai. My older brother was a member of a group of rebels who refused to pay the Raja's taxes, or to join the ranks of his army. When I was fourteen, I joined them. We lived in the forest and kept watch for Ramachandra's nobles or for a group of soldiers to pass through. When they did, we would surround them and force them to give up their horses and whatever wealth they had with them. In this way we harrassed the Raja and managed to go on living.

"Raja Ramchandra did not like it. He sent a force of eighty-four cavalrymen to seek us out in the forest and to either kill us or take us back in irons. We were only fifteen or twenty men, but we knew the forest and we had been told of their coming. So we set a trap. All of those men were trapped in a bog where their horses became stuck while we fired on them with arrows from the trees. Nearly all of the Raja's men were killed.

"Some time after that, I went to a festival at the temple in Ambodhia. I had always loved to attend the holiday festivals, and after that massacre, I felt the need to go there. While I was there, a poor woman came around begging money. She had scarcely any clothes on her body, and she was carrying a sick and hungry child. So I gave her a few coins, and asked her how she came to be in such a state. She told me she had not always been so. She said she had been a rich woman, married to an officer in the Raja's cavalry, but that a few months ago he had been killed along with his entire squad of men when he had gone into the forest to hunt down some rebels. And that now she was a widow with no one to look after her, and had to sleep on the ground and beg for her food.

"After that, I felt terrible; for I knew that I had been among those responsible for her condition. I went into the temple with a sickness in my heart. I wanted to die. It was a Kali temple; I grabbed the sword of Kali and cut my throat with it, in a fit of despair." So saying, Namadev pulled open his shirt and showed a long red scar along the side of his neck.

"The blood was flying all over the temple and the priests began screaming at me that I was polluting the temple, and they caught me and threw me out. My friends came then, and took me away and bandaged my neck. I had resolved to die, to atone for this life of killing; but I had failed to die. I felt that the Lord had spared me for some reason. I then resolved to spend the rest of my life repenting of my deeds and praying to God. And so I have come to Pandharpur, to seek God's mercy, and to give my life to Him."

Jnaneshvar was astonished at Namadev's story, but at the same time he was filled with loving compassion for this brave young man. "I've heard it said," he told Namadev, "that it is those whom the Lord most loves that he most severely tests. And He must love you since He filled your heart with love for Him and brought you to this heavenly place."

"Yes," said Namadev; "I believe that. Now I spend my time writing songs to Hari. Would ycu care to hear one of my songs?"

Jnaneshvar expressed his eagerness to hear one, and Namadev began to sing:

> O Lord, Thy name is this blind man's staff;
> Poor and wretched, Lord, I have no support
> but Thy name.
>
> Merciful and compassionate, Thou art my
> bountiful Lord;
> Ever-present before me, Thou pervadest
> all things.
>
> Thou art the ocean of beneficence,
> showering infinite wealth.
> Thou art both the giver and the taker;
> there is none else but Thee.
>
> How may I know Thee? Thou Thyself
> art my wisdom and my vision.
> O ever-forgiving God, Thou art Nama's
> beloved Lord. [16]

Jnaneshvar became filled with emotion as he sat listening to Namadev's song. Choked with happiness, he sat still for a long while, holding Nama's hand between his own two. "I believe," said Jnaneshvar, "that one day He will reveal Himself to you, and you will awaken His love in the hearts of many others through your beautiful songs."

"Do you think so?"

Jnandev smiled; "I know so," he said. And from that time on, he and Namadev were fast friends.

III

In time, Jnaneshvar became the center of a small group of devotees and was regarded as a sort of boy-wonder among them. He was revered as much for his personal sweetness and compassion with those around him as he was for his superior learning and divine experiences. His devotional songs became well known and were copied out and sung in the temples. In this way, his name became known to a large segment of those who frequented the evening *kirtana* in the temple; and often when he spoke with a few young men about the need to know God as their own innermost Self, the crowd would inevitably expand as the devout gathered to hear the words of the young saint in their midst.

Among those closest to Jnandev were, of course, his immediate family, and Namadev, who was perhaps his dearest friend; and then there was Vishobha Kechar, who was Guru to Namadev; and Gora, who had been a potter in the town of Teradhokhi; and Choka, a bricklayer from Sangli, who was an untouchable. And there was also Samvata, a gardener; Narahari, a goldsmith; and Janabai, the maidservant to Namadev, who also composed songs of love to her Lord.

Together, this group of young men and women formed a corps of earnest lovers of God around whom many others found great joy. During the day, they worked at their trades, and at night they gathered in the temple to sing, to chant God's name to the sound of drums and tamburas, flutes and tambourines. For much of the night they would rock joyfully in the waves of song, on the ocean of sweetness, till in the early hours of the morning, they would at last make their way happily homeward.

IV

One day, Jnaneshvar received a letter from a yogi by the name of Changadev, who lived nearby in the hills outside Pandharpur. Changadev was perhaps the most famous, and, reputedly, the most powerful, ascetic in all of Maharashtra. He was said to possess great wealth and a very large following of disciples, who regarded him as a supernatural being, a *Siddha*, whose extraordinary occult powers could accomplish whatever he wished. When Jnaneshvar was told that the letter handed to him was from the great Changadev, he was quite surprised and also delighted. No doubt Changadev had heard of him, just as he had heard of Changadev. 'Perhaps he is proposing a meeting,' thought Jnandev as he unsealed the letter. But when he had opened it, he found only a blank sheet. There was nothing written on it at all! For some time, Jnaneshvar thought about this, and then he discussed it with his brother, Nivritti.

"No doubt the man is challenging you to a sort of game," said Nivritti.

"A game? What do you mean?"

"You see, Changadev, the great yogi, who is revered by his devotees as a god, has heard about this young fellow called Jnaneshvar, and he is curious; yet, at the same time, he must be cautious, he must preserve his dignity and superiority. How would it look if so great a man were to write to so young a man seeking a meeting. Some would say he was seeking your favor. So, while he has sent you a letter, he has not sent you a letter. Don't you see?"

Jnaneshvar smiled. "Yes, I think you are right. But I have no reputation to uphold; I will answer his letter. And I will ask him to come and meet us. What do you think?"

"I think that would be good," said Nivritti. "Speak to him with great respect and reverence, with the awareness that he is the very manifestation of God, that he is your very own Self, and he will feel great love for us. Perhaps, then, he will come to visit us."

"Yes. Thank you, my brother; that is just what I shall do," said Jnandev. And he gathered up his writing materials and sat down to write his reply to Changadev (See the *Changadev Pasashti,* "Letter To Changadev," in Book Two of this volume).

It was several weeks later, after their morning meditation and prayers in the temple, that Jnaneshvar, Nivritti, Sopan and Muktabai, having taken a short walk to the edge of town, were sitting on a low stone wall, talking and enjoying the cool morning air. Having so recently come from their meditations in the temple, they were all feeling very light-headed and gay, still immersed in the sweetness of contemplation.

In the distance, a small group of travellers could be seen approaching the city of Pandharpur on foot along the dusty road. As the group approached nearer, it became apparent that the large, barrel-chested man in the lead was a yogi, and that the others were his followers. This very stalwart and impressive looking yogi wore the skin of a tiger on his body and his hair was piled on top of his head, intertwined with strands of rudraksha beads. He wore a full beard sprinkled with white, and the three white ash-marks of Shiva on his forehead, with a vermillion streak between his eyebrows.

Jnaneshvar leapt down from his seat on the wall, and the others followed. They stood respectfully beside the entrance to the city to salute and welcome the handsome yogi and his entourage. With their hands held palms-together at their chests, they bowed their heads in the traditional *namaskar* as he drew near. The yogi paused and stopped before the youngsters. "Om namah Shivaya," said Jnaneshvar; "we welcome you to the city of Pandharpur."

"I thank you," said the yogi. "Perhaps you can tell me where I might find the dwelling of a young man called Jnaneshvar, the poet."

"Certainly I could, sir," said Jnaneshvar, "since I am Jnaneshvar."

"But it is you I have come to meet!" exclaimed the yogi. "I am Changadev."

"But it is you we have come to meet!" said Jnandev. And everyone there laughed, as the two men stood beaming at each other. "Perhaps," said Jnandev, "it is Hari who has arranged to meet Himself in this way by bringing us together."

Everyone smiled in agreement to this, as Jnaneshvar and Changadev embraced lovingly. Then, after introducing his family to Changadev, Jnaneshvar invited him and his entourage to their humble dwelling where a large feast was prepared. It was only later, as they sat in the shade of a huge neem tree, that Changadev revealed the purpose of his visit:

"My dear brother," he began, "I was greatly moved by your wonderful letter; and I have come to invite you to join me in a pilgrimage to Kashi. At *amavashya,* the New Moon of October, I will depart for the north; I will pass through Prayag, Gaya, and other holy *tirthas* on my way. I am taking a number of people with me in my company, and I would be greatly honored if you and your gracious family would join me as my guests."

"Benares ..." mused Jnandev. He was thinking of the tales his father had told of the glorious city on the Ganges, and of the dream his father had of one day taking his sons to that holy city. "How long will you be gone?" asked Jnaneshvar.

"Perhaps a year; perhaps longer," Changadev replied.

"And I must mention also that this journey is not without dangers. The Khalji rulers have swarmed over much of these northern lands, and everywhere we will meet with unfriendly and alien peoples. It will not be an easy journey."

Jnandev cast a quick glance at Nivritti; then he said, "It is very kind of you to invite us, holy father. We are very happy that you have thought to include us in your plans. Let us discuss this idea amongst ourselves, and I will give you an answer."

"Of course, my son," said Changadev. We will stay the night in Pandharpur and will leave at dawn. You have plenty of time to talk it over. And tonight you could perhaps show me your famous temple and your equally famous *kirtana*."

"It will be my greatest happiness, dear Changadeva. And I shall introduce you to my friends. You will love them, and they will be equally delighted to meet you."

Later that night, Namadev and his maidservant, Janabai, were also invited to join the pilgrimage. And after much discussion among them, it was decided; they would go. And so, on the New Moon of October, 1295, Jnaneshvar, Nivritti, Sopan and Muktabai, along with Namadev and Janabai, gathered in the temple of Vithoba to ask Krishna's blessing on their long journey. It was still early in the morning when they set out from Pandharpur to join Changadev and his company on their great adventure into the north country.

11 ON THE ROAD TO KASHI

It was a dangerous time to travel so far into the territories ruled by the Muslim Sultanate. The roads were teeming with *dacoits*, and revolution and warfare were rampant throughout the land. The large number of people in Changadev's party, and their noticeable impoverishment no doubt served in their favor to discourage *dacoits* and to offer no temptation to greedy rulers of the various principalities through which they passed. They were merely a band of harmless ascetics, religious itinerants, who offered neither threat nor advantage to anyone; and so they were free to go along their way with no trouble from anyone.

Still, as they passed through the troubled land, they witnessed, in the faces of the people and in the ruined towns, the violence which had afflicted the country. They came across many hundreds of people whose lands had been invaded, whose temples had been desecrated and pulled down, whose shops had been pillaged, whose children had been murdered or enslaved. And whenever they could, they offered food and clothing to those widows and children who were the victims of these acts.

Benares had long been in the hands of the Muslim invaders, since it was first taken by the Ghurid general, Bakhtyar Khalji in the year 1206; and it had frequently been in the hands of the Sultanate since that time. Now, as they neared the holy city of Benares on the Ganges, they were entering deeply into territory ruled by the Muslim conquerors.

One evening, as the group of travellers made camp beside the Ganges, a lone man approached them on foot. He was old and his clothing was tattered, but still the ochre color of the cloth showed plainly. He was a *sannyasin*, a wandering monk, and he looked very hungry and weary. The man was invited to share their evening meal and the hospitality of their camp for the night, and as the pilgrims talked with the sannyasin, they learned that he had come recently from the town of Bhilsa, near Chandheri. He had been serving as an assistant to the priests in a large temple there when Ala-uddin Khalji had sacked the city. And now he wandered southward along the banks of the Ganges, hoping to escape the Muslim armies. While the women prepared their meal, the men gathered around the old sannyasin to hear his tale.

"All the temples in our land have fallen into neglect," he said; "worship in them has stopped. Within their walls the frightful howls of the jackals have taken the place of the sweet reverberations of the mridunga. The sweet fragrance of the smoke of the homa-fire and the chanting of the Vedas have deserted the villages which are now filled with the foul smell of roasted flesh and the fierce noise of the ruffian *Turushkas* (Turkish Muslims). The beautiful gardens of the cities now present a most painful sight; many of their beautiful cocoanut palms have been cut down; and on every side are seen rows of stakes from which swing strings of human skulls. The rivers flow red with the blood of the slaughtered cows. The Veda is forgotten, and justice has gone into hiding; there is not left any trace of virtue or nobility in the land and despair is written large on the faces of India's unfortunate people. [17]

"The wicked *mlechhas* pollute the religion of the Hindus every day. They break the images of the gods into pieces and throw the articles of worship into the garbage pits. They throw the *Srimad Bhagavatam* and other scriptures into the fire, forcibly take away the conch and bell of the brahmin priests, and lick the sandal-paste marks from the women's bodies. They urinate like dogs on the sacred Tulsi plant, and deliberately pass feces on the altars of our temples. They spit upon the Hindus engaged in worship, and harass the Hindu saints as if they were so many lunatics on the loose. [18]

"With my own eyes, I saw them put a good woman to the test of faith. She had been accused of teaching the Hindu faith, and it was declared that she would be tried by having four large pots of water tied to her hands and feet, and then she would be thrown into the deepest part of the river. If she drowned, she would be ruled innocent. But she did not drown; somehow she escaped and made her way to shore. By the terms of this trial, this was taken as proof that she was guilty as a *kaftar* (non-believer in Islam). The naib-us-sultan then ordered her to be burnt. This I saw with my own eyes. [19] Do you wonder that all our suffering people pray for the day when all of Aryavarta will be free of these murdering fiends! But, my friends, God does not hear us. I fear He has forsaken us."

All during the evening meal, the pilgrims were discussing among themselves what the old sannyasin had said. Jnaneshvar also pondered over what he had heard. He knew that all that occurred was ordained by God, was God's own actions; yet he could not understand why the Lord saw fit to cause such pain and sorrow on the earth. Later, after their meal, as they sat around the fire, the old sannyasin spoke again:

"The times have become very hard in our country," he said. "The Muslim tyrants with their ruthless armies of killers have taken the entire northern part of Bharadwaja, and have set up their kingdom in our sacred city of Delhi. Thousands of people are tortured and murdered daily. And I say it is only a matter of time before they cross the mountains and march on Devgiri itself. Then your people too will be slaughtered at Pandharpur, and your temples will be destroyed, your sisters raped and your children enslaved! Why should it be so, my dear friends? What can God have in mind to treat His people so?"

For a moment no one answered the old man; but finally, Changadev spoke up; "It is better not to question the ways of God," he said. "The law of karma is impenetrable; but the causes of every man's fruits in this life go back to lives before lives, and the cause of what comes to us now is lost in the deep recesses of the past, and cannot be known by the mind of man."

"Yes," said the sannyasin, "I know. I've heard all that myself. But look, if you go back to the causes of actions and you keep going back and back, musn't you eventually come to a beginning of all causes, and isn't that God Himself? Eh?"

Jnaneshvar chuckled; "I think he's got you there, dear Changadev; what do you say?"

"It seems to me," put in the sannyasin, "it's the noblest souls who suffer the most. Why? It's the ones who trust in God, who are good and gentle -- they are torn to pieces while the murderers grow fat, the liars get rich and the stupid grow more content. What of those good and honest men whom God tortures and drives to the river to drown themselves by their own hand in despair? What of the holy Shankara, or Isha?

God tortures such men. He leaves them no place to sleep, with nothing to eat, no friends to love, to laugh with; and when they speak of God, they are beaten and despised among men. Is this a loving God, to make such a world? I ask you!"

Everyone sat quietly gazing into the glowing embers of the fire. Nivritti then spoke; "I think we cannot judge from the point of view of human values, whether what God has done is good or bad. It is as it is, beyond our feeble notions of good and bad; and in the end, when all the yugas are passed and we come to the end of the kalpa, all will be seen to be perfect in the beginning, perfect in its unfolding, and perfect in its end."

"Perhaps," said the sannyasin, "but still I say that if God's world is one in which the good suffer more in proportion to their goodness, where the wise are reviled and the dull-witted are honored; where the gentle are persecuted and the mean are highly respected; where the seers are called 'mad' and the deluded are called 'great' -- then God has done badly, and His world is not fit to live in."

"That is one perspective," said Nivritti; "but if He secretly upholds the good with strength in their sufferings, and gives contentment to the wise in their solitary lives, and fills the hearts of the gentle with the joy of love, and grants to the seers the vision of Himself, the knowledge and bliss of the eternal Self -- then God has done well, and His world is a marvellous world."

The sannyasin remained silent. Jnaneshvar also said nothing. There was nothing more to be said; and so, one by one, the men wandered off to prepare their bedding for the night and to sit quietly beneath the stars, while nearby they could hear the voice of Muktabai, softly singing:

Rama Raghava, Rama Raghava
Rama Raghava, raksha mam
(Lord Rama, protect me)
Krishna Keshava, Krishna Keshava
Krishna Keshava, pahi mam
(Lord Krishna, enlighten me)

12 RETURN TO PANDHARPUR

After almost exactly one year from the date of their departure, Jnaneshvar and his family, along with Namadev and Janabai, returned to Pandharpur. Arriving in the early evening, they went directly to the temple to prostrate at the feet of Vithoba. But they were so exhausted from the last leg of their journey that they didn't bother to eat their evening meal, but went immediately to bed. For several days, they did nothing but rest. Then came the visitors. Everyone -- Gora, Choka, Sena, and the ladies from the temple -- arrived, one after another, to welcome them back to Pandharpur and to question them about their travels. It soon became apparent to everyone, however, that a profound change had come over their old friends, and that Jnandev, especially, seemed dramatically affected by the misery and distress he had witnessed on his journey.

He seemed no longer his old buoyant and exuberant self, but appeared very often listless and distracted. The entire family had been quite evidently affected very deeply by what they had seen in their travels into the world, and a great burden of weariness seemed to have afflicted the minds of each one of them. "Time," Muktabai insisted to her questioning friends, "will heal the hearts of my brothers. Let them rest; they're just very tired." And she continued, in her quietly efficient way, to look after the domestic chores and to serve her brothers cheerfully. Sopan managed to find some work, helping a nearby farmer, and each night brought home some rice, flour, or vegetables to supply the family's needs.

Jnandev returned to the temple and resumed his nightly *kirtana*, but in his own heart there remained a heaviness which the songs that once inspired him with joy could not eradicate. Time and again, he told himself how foolish he was to allow such a gloomy mood to overtake his mind, but he seemed powerless to dispel it. It seemed as though whatever taste for life he had once possessed, had now vanished, and existence itself had become valueless, even burdensome.

Nivritti, aware of his brother's state of mind, and aware also of the need to draw him once again into the business of life, insisted that Jnandev resume his classes on the *Bhagavad Gita*, using his own commentaries from his *Bhavarthaaipika* written five years earlier to explain its meaning to his students. This, despite his disinterest, Jnaneshvar agreed to do.

It was just about this time, in early April of 1296, that word was received in Pandharpur that within a day's ride, the Rani of Devgiri and her son, the prince Singhana, along with a large escort of troops, were on their way to the city of Pandharpur. It seemed that the queen, who was very devout in her religious feelings, had decided at this time to journey all this way from the palace at Devgiri to worship in the renowned temple of Vithoba.

There was great excitement in the city. Not since Raja Ramadev himself had come to visit Pandharpur twenty years before, in 1276, had the city been called upon to entertain the royal family. It had been requested that a *yajna* be held in their honor and that religious ceremonies be performed in the temple of Vithoba by the brahmin priests, with scriptural readings by the local pandits. It was also necessary to prepare housing and provisions, not only for the royal family, but for the nobles and soldiers in their company as well. Much needed to be done. Banners were hung above the housetops lining the entrance to the city; temple musicians were gathered; priests made hurried plans for the *yajna*; food was requisitioned from the farmers; and couriers were sent out to carry the word for miles around that the royal family was coming to Pandharpur.

The news came to Jnandev from Choka, who burst into their house with the excited announcement that the priests of the temple had requested Jnaneshvar to take part in the religious ceremonies by reciting a portion from his Marathi commentaries on the Gita; and they also wanted Muktabai to sing some of her songs as well. "I saw Mukti outside and told her all about it," Choka gasped, still trying to catch his breath.

Jnandev glanced across the room to Nivritti; he knew he would have to do it. "When?" he asked.

"Sometime tomorrow! They say she's coming with young Singhana, the future Raja, and more than a thousand troops!"

"A thousand? Why so many?"

"I dunno. Maybe they were expecting trouble on

the way. Who knows? Anyway, we have to be there tomorrow when they all arrive."

"I'll be there. You can tell the priests we'll be be there," said Jnandev, glancing once again at Nivritti who seemed to be amused.

"I have to go tell Namdev and the others!" said Choka on his way out. "Come directly to the temple when they arrive. They will tell you when you are to do your reading. OK?"

"Yes, yes. I'll be there."

"OK. See you there!" And Choka rushed out the door and down the road to spread the news.

On the following day, Jnandev stood alongside the street with the crowded citizens of Pandharpur, watching the Rani's royal entrance into the city. A few hundred troops preceded her, as she was carried in a jeweled palanquin by eight muscular attendants. She was sitting proudly upright, wearing a flowing white sari and a diadem of pearls, as she waved to the waiting crowd and received a welcoming cheer. Jnandev was impressed by her elegant beauty and by the kindliness revealed in her face. Behind her on a white charger rode the crown prince, Singhana -- about his own age, Jnandev guessed, but a very proud peacock indeed. He wore a silver-brocaded jacket and a red silk turban, at his side a gleaming gold sword scabbard with a jeweled hilt.

Jnandev had never seen so many soldiers. As the parade of visitors wound up the narrow street the line of armed horsemen seemed endless. After watching for awhile, he made his way to the temple where the ceremonies would be held. There he made his way through the crowded hall and took his place beside Muktabai among the musicians and brahmin priests seated near the statue of Vithoba.

When the Rani appeared through the throng at the door with the prince at her side, she was led to the foot of the *murti* of Krishna, where she and the prince went to their knees, touching their heads to the marble floor. When they were seated, the priests ended their low chanting of the Vedas, and the musicians seated near Jnandev began their program, as Muktabai, beautiful as an angel in her borrowed silk sari, began to sing her plaintive songs.

When Muktabai had finished with the third song --

a long representation of Radha's longing for Krishna -- it was Jnaneshvar's turn. He opened the large bound volume before him, and began to recite from his own work:

> *O man, you are indeed sitting in a wrecked boat with a hundred holes in it. How can you hope to find comfort on this perilous journey?*
> *Life is indeed a fair, where the wares of misery are being spread out and allocated by fate.*
> *When you see that a conflagration is surrounding you in a forest, would it not be an act of prudence on your part to get out of it as quickly as possible?*
> *You are sleeping on a bed of scorpions. How can you hope to sleep in comfort and peace?*

Just as the recitation had begun, a guard from the prince's retinue who had been positioned at the temple-doorway received a message from another soldier. For a moment, they were engaged in an excited exchange, attracting some curious attention from many of the people seated nearby.

> *Avaricious and inconsiderate, you are like a frog trying to eat a fish while it is itself being devoured by a large snake. All things in this world are transitory; even the moon is each month consumed. Stars rise in this world only in order to set, and birth only means the certainty of death.*

The guard came forward, making his way hurriedly to the side of prince Singhana. Kneeling, he whispered something which appeared to startle the prince. Again there was an excited exchange. Those who had watched this chain of events were intrigued; 'what,' they wondered, 'could be so important among princes and guards to warrant causing a disturbance in the temple of Vithoba?'

> *Parents, though they know that their children are only approaching nearer to death, cele-*

> *brate the day marking the passage of each year with great joy. Death indeed is like a lion's den to which all steps lead, but from which none return.*

Then the prince leaned over to the Rani and whispered something to her. Clearly, something was very wrong; the Rani was obviously alarmed. By now, nearly everyone in the temple -- except for Jnaneshvar, who continued to read -- knew that something was greatly amiss.

> *History is merely the record of dead men. Why do not these considerations prompt you, O vile man, to the pursuit of spiritual life? The whole world is full of misery. Who has ever heard a tale of happiness in this mortal world? If you have been so unfortunate as to have born in this world, your first endeavor should be to get out of it as quickly as possible by making God the object of your devotion and effort.*

Now, the prince stood up quickly and helped the Rani to her feet. He led her hurriedly to the doorway and outside. A murmuring arose around the doorway, and voices were heard shouting excitedly outside. By now everyone in the packed crowd inside the temple had turned 'round to find out what was going on. Jnandev had stopped his recitation, and was wondering, with everyone else, what could be the excitement, when someone stepped inside the doorway and announced in a loud voice which everyone could hear: "The Sultan's army is attacking the palace at Devgiri!"

13 THE SEIGE OF DEVGIRI

It was on Saturday, February 26, 1296, that Ala-uddin left Kera with a mere 8000 horsemen, ostensibly headed for Chandheri. He had used this same road before, when he had ridden with his troops to the town of Bhilsa, and so, confident of the security of the roads, he made haste with his troops toward Chandheri. But just before he reached that city, he turned his men directly southward toward the Vindhya and Satpura mountain ranges. Forcing his cavalry along at a rapid pace, he led them across the Vindhya mountains along narrow pathways and over rugged uncharted terrain. Finally, after making his way through dense jungles and across swift rivers, he arrived at Ellichpur, the northernmost outpost of the Yadava dominions; and there he stopped, in order to allow his men to rest from their long hard journey and to prepare for the battle ahead.

By this time, of course, their presence had been discovered by the neighboring populace; and to put them off of his real intentions, Ala-uddin sent abroad the rumor that he had rebelled against the Sultan in Delhi and was heading southeast to seek refuge in the service of the Raja of Rajmundri in Telingana, a vassalage of the Yadava king on the eastern coast. This subterfuge seemed to work well, for he and his troops were left to travel in peace.

But it was not long before they were on the march again toward Devgiri, and not long before Ramchandra's spies brought word to him that Ala-uddin's men had attacked and routed the forces of one of his chieftans, Kanha, at Lasaura, about 12 miles to the northwest of Devgiri, and were now headed toward the city. Ramadev immediately sent out his soldiers -- only three or four thousand strong --, but they were quickly beaten back to the citadel within the city. Unfortunately, a large segment of Devgiri's battle troops had left the fortress some days ago, led by the king's elder son, Singhana, to accompany the Rani to Pandharpur where she had gone in order to worship the famous *murti* of Krishna.

No one had even imagined that the Muslims at Delhi would dare such a bold attack. Devgiri had never been attacked in all its hundred-year history; its fortress was impregnable. Who could have anticipated that anyone would think of challenging it? There was nothing for Ramchandra to do under the circumstances but to fortify himself and his small remaining forces within the walls of the fortress and hope to hold off the invaders until his son returned with reinforcements.

Meanwhile, Ala-uddin and his men swept into the lower town which was unguarded by walls, and took many of the merchants and wealthy citizens as hostages. He also captured forty elephants and a thousand horses from the royal stables. Then he sent a message to the beseiged king that he and his 8000 men were only a vanguard; the rest of the Sultan's army, he told them -- some 20,000 horsemen -- were just behind him and would be arriving shortly. At this news, Ramchandra lost all hope; he had only a small store of provisions, and not enough men to withstand such an attack anyway, and so he sued for peace, offering to satisfy the demands of a treaty. He offered the sum of fifty *maunds* [20] of gold and a quantity of pearls and other jewels, advising Ala-uddin that he would do well to accept this offer. In his letter to him he wrote:

> Your invasion of this city was imprudent and rash; but fortunately for you, you found the city unguarded, and you have been permitted to range at large. It is, however, possible that the Rajas of the Deccan, who command innumerable armies, may yet surround you and not permit one of your people to return from our dominions alive. Supposing, even, that you should be able to retreat from hence undisturbed, are not the princes of Malwa, Kandeish and Gondwara in your route who have each armies of 40,000 or 50,000 men? Can you hope they will permit you to escape unmolested? It is advisable, therefore, for you to retire in time, by accepting a moderate sum, which, with the spoils you have already got, will indemnify you for the expense of your expedition. [21]

Ala-uddin considered these words; then he accepted

Ramchandra's proposal and payment of ransom, and agreed to release all his prisoners and leave within fifteen days, after giving his men some time to rest.

However, prince Singhana, having received news of his father's distress while at the temple of Pandharpur, hurried back to Devgiri with his own and some additional troops whom he gathered from neighboring chieftans on his return. As he approached the city, another messenger met him with news from his father that Ala-uddin had accepted his treaty and was about to leave, and that Singhana should do nothing to interfere as they could not hope to win in battle anyway. But Singhana, fired with the impetuosity of youth, confident that he had the larger force, and expecting the immanent arrival of more troop reinforcements from the surrounding territories, ignored his father's command, and sent a message of his own to Ala-uddin: "If you have any love for life," it read, "and desire safety, restore what you have plundered, and proceed quietly homeward, rejoicing at your happy escape."

Ala-uddin, infuriated by the young prince's audacity, divided his forces, leaving 1000 men behind under the command of his general, Malik Nasrat, to guard the fort so that Ramchandra's men might not join the battle as well, and set out with the other 7000 men to meet the young prince. But they had underestimated the cavalry of Singhana; the Muslim forces soon found themselves outnumbered by the Marathi warriors, and it seemed for a moment that Ala-uddin and his men would be slaughtered by the defenders of Devgiri. Perceiving this, Malik Nasrat, the general in charge of the 1000 troops stationed at the fortress, disobeyed Ala-uddin's orders, and, abandoning his post, led his men to rally in defense of Ala-uddin and his hard-pressed army.

Ala-uddin and his men, seeing the charge of the additional forces, took up the cry, "Reinforcements! The Sultan's troops have arrived!" And Singhana's men, thinking that these 1000 charging warriors were indeed the spearhead of the 20,000-man force of which Ala-uddin had boasted, turned tail, and fled the battlefield. Devgiri, once again, had been conquered by a ruse. This time, Ala-uddin, revitalized by his conquest, renewed his attack upon the fortress with a vengeance, and killed many of the merchants and citizens whom he had previously taken as prisoners -- some of whom were the king's own relatives --, and paraded their bodies in front of the fortress gates. It was also at this time that Ramadev learned that the sacks, thought to contain grain, which had been hurriedly gathered inside the fortress at the onset of the attack, contained not grain, but salt. And so, Ramchandra and his few men, for whom there was no food provisioned for a siege, had no choice but to meet the demands of a new treaty.

To fulfil this treaty, Ala-uddin demanded the acession of the outlying territory of Ellichpur and its dependencies, and a ransom of 600 maunds of gold; two maunds each of diamonds, rubies, pearls, emeralds and sapphires; 1000 maunds of silver, and 4000 bolts of varicolored silk. He would also have one of the king's daughters as his wife to assure good future relations. Thus, just twenty-five days after he had arrived in Devgiri, Ala-uddin departed for his return to Kera, the captured elephants and horses laden with the better part of Devgiri's precious treasure of gold, silver, and jewels, as well as silks and countless other articles of value. Furthermore, according to their treaty, the city of Eilichpur, including its yearly revenues, now belonged to Ala-uddin, with an additional tithe to be paid yearly from Ramchandra's treasury. Also accompanying Ala-uddin was his new wife, the king's daughter, Princess Jhatiapali, as he made his triumphant return back across the mountains to Kera, where he arrived on June 3, 1296.

About this eminently successful expedition of Ala-uddin's, the 16th century historian, Ferishta, remarks, "in the long volumes of history, there is scarcely anything to be compared with this exploit, where we regard the resolution in forming the plan, the boldness of its execution, or the great good fortune which attended its accomplishment." [22]

14 TREACHERY AT MANUKPUR

The Sultan, Jalal-uddin Khalji, who had been on an expedition of his own to Gwalior on the Jumna, had heard no word from his nephew for six months, and was beginning to be anxious for his safety. Then rumors reached him that Ala-uddin had captured not Chandheri, but Devgiri; and was returning to Kera with a treasure the likes of which no eyes had ever seen. At first, Jalal-uddin was overjoyed at this news, but his counsellors quickly reminded him that his nephew had deceived and betrayed him, and advised that he be cautious in dealing with him.

The Sultan thereupon called a meeting of his most trusted counsellors and asked them what was the appropriate thing to do in such a case. Should he ride to meet his nephew en route, before he arrived back in Kera, or should he just wait at Delhi for Ala-uddin to come on his own?

The counsellors were divided; one Mulik Ahmud Hubib suggested to the Sultan that his nephew was up to no good, and that he should send out a large army to meet him while he was yet on his way. Another, Mulik Fukir-uddin Kuchi, advised that the Sultan wait, allowing his nephew to return to Kera, and then see what he does after that. "Since the Sultan has the superior force," he said, "he could always give assault later on if it became necessary." The first counsel, Ahmad Hubib, retorted that as soon as Ala-uddin returned to Kera, he would no doubt proceed immediately to the remote province of Bengal, where, with his newly acquired wealth, he could easily set up his own kingdom and his own defenses.

The Sultan, however, was naively fond of his nephew, and refused to hear any such suspicions about him. "We are so well assured of the loyalty of Ala-uddin," he said, "that we would sooner believe treason of our own son than of him." And so the old Sultan returned to Delhi to await word from his nephew.

Soon after his arrival there, a letter came from Ala-uddin, stating that all the wealth he brought back from Devgiri belonged to the Sultan, but, he begged, as he was so exhausted from his long campaign, might he be allowed some little repose at Kera before bringing all that treasure to Delhi. He added that he was well-aware that he had enemies at court who had no doubt poisoned his uncle's mind against him, encouraging him to mete out some punishment to himself for his failure to apprise the Sultan of his intention to raid Devgiri. He therefore requested of the Sultan a letter of royal pardon, assuring him and his followers of their safety and of the Sultan's favor; and he signed it, "your devoted slave."

Ala-uddin then engaged his brother, Almas Beg, who was living at court in Delhi, to act as his go-between with the Sultan. He sent letters to the Sultan by way of his brother, expressing regret for his own shameful behavior in having gone to Devgiri without his uncle's permission, and stating his conviction that the Sultan would surely arrest him and slay him as soon as he rode into Delhi. He begged his brother, therefore, to intercede for him with the Sultan, to assure his uncle of his heart-felt remorse. He added that, if he was not immediately assured of his uncle's forgiveness, he would end his own life. Almas Beg then showed these sorrowful letters to the Sultan, thereby convincing him that, owing to Ala-uddin's irrational fear of coming to Delhi, he should go himself to Kera to offer his nephew his personal assurances.

Assenting to this plan, the Sultan embarked with a thousand mounted troops and a small retinue which accompanied him down the Jumna river. They met Ala-uddin at Manukpur on July 19, 1296. Ala-uddin was accompanied by his entire army who were there, he said, as an honor guard to salute the Sultan. Almas Beg informed the Sultan that his brother, Ala-uddin, was still quite fearful of his uncle's anger, and would be even more alarmed if he were approached by the 1000 troops; therefore, perhaps it would be best if the Sultan met with Ala-uddin accompanied only by his small retinue. And, ... ah yes, perhaps it would be best if his retinue left their armor and weapons behind, so as not to fuel Ala-uddin's suspicion that his uncle was out to get him. Some of the Sultan's retinue, beginning to suspect treachery, objected vehemently, but Almas Beg explained the situation so plausibly and with such apparent solicitation for the easing of his brother's mind, that they at last relented.

When the Sultan reached the landing place, Ala-uddin, leaving his attendants behind, went to meet his uncle alone, and fell prostrate at his feet. The old man lifted him up, caressing his cheek, and embraced him, saying, "How could you be suspicious of me, who have brought you up from childhood, and cherished you with a fatherly affection, holding you dearer in my sight, if possible, than my own offspring?"

Then he took his nephew by the hand, and began to lead him back to the royal barge, when Ala-uddin made a signal to his guards who were just behind them. One of the guards, Mahmud bin Salim, rushed forward and swung his sword downward. The blow fell on the Sultan's shoulder, and the Sultan, stumbling, and realizing that he had walked into a trap, began running for the barge, crying out, "Ah! you villain, Ala-uddin!" But before he could reach the barge, another of Ala-uddin's guards, Yektyar-uddin, caught the old man, threw him to the ground, and lopped off his head with his sword.

After the Sultan's attendants had also been slain, the head of the Sultan was stuck on the end of a spear and carried first through the camp and then through the cities of Manukpur, Kera, and Oudh. Later, the royal canopy of the Sultan was raised over the head of Ala-uddin, the new Sultan of India, with great ceremony and pomp. Ala-uddin cautiously bided his time at Kera for some months thereafter, and recruited a large army of 60,000 horsemen, purchased with his newly acquired wealth. Then, on October 22, 1296, at the height of the rainy season, he rode triumphantly into Delhi and took up his residence in the Red Palace as Sultan Ala-uddin Khalji.

15 JNANESHVAR'S SAMADHI

In November of 1296, while Ala-uddin was consolidating his power at Delhi, Jnaneshvar and his friends met in the temple of Vithoba, during the festival of *Karttika-ekadashi*, and joined in the chanting of God's name to the music of tambouras, mridungs and hand-cymbals; but none of them could help thinking that the end of everything they loved at Pandharpur was at hand. Soon the marauding Muslim armies would come; and already most of the young men of the city were joining the ranks of the local warrior chieftans, training for battle. Ramchandra and the impregnable fortress of Devgiri had been taken and sacked; how could they hope to stem the tide of these murdering hordes?

Jnaneshvar remained in the temple after the others had gone home. He felt the time had come to pray to Vithoba for some indication of what he must do. For, it seemed, the joyous days and nights at Pandharpur which surpassed even the joys of heaven were no more to be. The sweet pleasure of hearing the laughter of the ingenuous Choka, of seeing the unbridled love in the eyes of Namadev, of listening to the voice of Gora, which rivalled that of the Gandarvas -- how was it possible that these sounds and sights would soon be replaced in Pandharpur by the sound of swords clashing, the sight of murderous hatred in the eyes of evil men, and of the blood of innocent and gentle people flowing in the streets?

Everything, he felt certain, would be destroyed. There was still time to flee; but where would he go? Wouldn't it be far better to die now, after so beautiful a life, with such sweet memories of love, and the peaceful awareness of God, than to live on and see the world spoiled and raped? 'Has not this life already been enjoyed to the full?' thought Jnandev. 'Is it not time for me to shed this body and reclaim my eternal bliss? Is this not truly what I wish above all? Yes, truly. I have no fear; why then should I not take leave of my friends now while love still shines in our eyes instead of fear and anguish?'

"Dear Lord," Jnaneshvar whispered, "is not my work finished? May I return to Thee?" And with the very thought of giving up the limitations inherent in bodily existence, he felt such an overwhelming sense of freedom and relief, such a wave of bliss and expansiveness, that all doubts were swept away. "O merciful Lord! I have fulfilled the purpose of my life; I have given what I had to give, and now I shall return to Thee!"

In the morning, Jnaneshvar, still seated at the feet of Krishna in the temple, met his brothers and sister and friends. There he told them of his plan. He told them that he was going to enter his final *samadhi*, and that, having spoken with his Lord during the night, he had received the inspiration to return to Alandi and cast off his body there, near the temple of Siddheshvar.

"No, Jnani!" exclaimed Muktabai; "you cannot! I forbid it!"

"Listen," said Jnandev, "we must all die sometime. Surely you have recognized this fact. For me, it is the time. It is a matter for great joy, not for sadness. I shall die as a man should die -- willingly and with great happiness and satisfaction." He took Muktabai's hand in his own. "Dear sister, my brothers, understand me; I long only for my true freedom and rest in God. There is nothing at all here that could give me even the least kind of satisfaction. I can think of nothing here at all that could please me.

"I have done what I wished to do, and what I was meant to do; I have written my books, and I have shared everything with all of you. There is nothing left for me to do here. I have determined to leave. The rest of you may do as you wish. It would make me very happy, though, if all of you would accompany me to Alandi; we will have a great celebration, and I will leave this world with those I love surrounding me. With your loving thoughts near me, I shall surely ascend to God."

There was nothing that could be said to dissuade him. And so, stunned and saddened as they were, his friends and family accompanied Jnaneshvar to Alandi. There, by his instructions, Gora, Choka and others built a small rectangular crypt of brick and mortar facing the holy temple of Siddheshvara, while, for seven days and nights, the chanting of God's name resounded throughout Alandi. On the day Jnaneshvar had chosen for his departure (the 13th day of the dark half of

Karttika; around the first week of December, 1296), the crypt was lined with flowers, and a deerskin was spread on the floor.

The chanting had reached its pinnacle and ended. The *purnahuti*, the auspicious hour, had come. Jnaneshvar arose, and approached the entrance to the crypt. One by one, his brothers, sister, and friends stepped forward to embrace and kiss him one last time. The garlands of flowers they placed 'round his neck were drenched with tears. Then, saluting them all with a final *namaskar*, a heavenly inebriation shining on his face, Jnandev entered into the small hut-like crypt. Seating himself on the deerskin in the yogic posture, and placing his beloved *Jnaneshvari* close by, he sat quietly, repeating the name of God within his heart; then he signalled to Nivritti, and the heavy stone door was closed in place.

Once the door was sealed, there was only silence. Then many fell down weeping, crying out in their loneliness and pain. A large crowd, along with the brothers, Muktabai, Namadev and Janabai, stayed to keep a silent vigil outside the crypt into the night. As they sat, looking bewilderedly at the small shrine by firelight, gradually it dawned in the minds of each of them that their friend and brother, the very soul of God, who, for twenty-five years, lived and spoke and laughed before them, was now gone forever. And yet each of them knew, also, that Jnaneshvar, who had been a brother and friend, now filled the earth and the heavens, and radiated his love and wisdom to all the world.

POSTSCRIPT

Within a month after Jnaneshvar's self-immolation, his brothers and sister had also taken their own lives. Sopan, the youngest, gave up his life at Saswad, a few miles west of Alandi; Muktabai vanished somewhere along the banks of the Tapti river; and Nivritti ended his life at Triambakeshvar in the region of Nasik. Namadev lived to the ripe old age of eighty. Some say he remained at Pandharpur; others say he spent much of his life in northern India, wandering from region to region, until finally settling in a small village called Ghuman in the Punjab, and that only toward the end of his life did he return to Pandharpur. In any event, his bones were buried in front of the Vithoba temple, next to Chokhamela's, and remain there to this day.

The two assasins of Sultan Jalal-uddin Khalji died particularly unpleasant deaths within a year after their treacherous deed. The first one, Malik bin Salim, died of a horrible leprosy which dissolved his flesh piecemeal from his bones; the other, Yektyar-uddin, went raving mad, crying out to the end that the Sultan was trying to cut off his head.

As for Ala-uddin, he lived to rule at Delhi for twenty years, proving his ability to defend his realm from the repeated attacks of the Mongols from the north, and to reduce the Hindu populace to a state of utter submission. The latter he did so well that, as his legal officer, Qazi Mughis-uddin, stated, "If the revenue collector spits into a Hindu's mouth, the Hindu must open his mouth to receive it without hesitation." The historian, Barani, who was contemporary with Ala-uddin's reign, said that according to the Sultan's orders,

> ...The Hindu was to be so reduced as to be unable to keep a horse, wear fine clothes, or enjoy any of life's luxuries. No Hindu could hold up his head, and in their houses no sign of gold or silver or any superfluity was to be seen. These things, which were thought to nourish insubordination, were not to be found. ... The people were oppressed and amerced, and money was exacted from them, on every kind of pretext.

> All pensions, grants of land, and endowments were appropriated. The people became so absorbed in trying to keep themselves alive that rebellion was never even mentioned.
>
> Next, [Sultan Ala-uddin] set up so minute a system of espionage that nothing done, good or bad, was hidden from him. No one could stir without his knowledge, and whatever happened in the houses of his own nobles, grandees and officials was brought by his spies for his information, and their reports were acted upon. To such a length did this prying go that nobles dared not speak aloud even in thousand-columned palaces, but had to communicate by signs. In their own houses, night and day, dread of the spies made them tremble. What went on in the bazaars was also reported and controlled. [23]

At one time during his career, Ala-uddin Khalji decided to start a new religion, with himself as its Messiah, and to conquer the entire world as Alexander had done. He even had coins minted with the title, 'Alexander II' stamped under his own likeness. He then gave up that idea and began instead the less ambitious territorial conquest of the southern part of India. An admiring historian writes in the *Tarikh-i-Wassaf*:

> With a view to holy war, and not merely for the lust of conquest, [Ala-uddin] enlisted ... about 14,000 cavalry and 20,000 infantry. The Muhammedan forces began to kill and slaughter on the right and on the left unmercifully throughout the land, for the sake of Islam, and blood flowed in torrents.
>
> They took captive a great number of handsome and elegant maidens, amounting to 20,000; and children of both sexes, more than the pen can enumerate. ... In short, the Muhammedan army brought the country to utter ruin, and destroyed the lives of

> the inhabitants, and plundered the cities, and captured their offspring so that many temples were deserted and the idols were broken and ... the fragments were conveyed to Delhi, where the entrance of the Jami Mosque was paved with them, so that people might remember and talk of this brilliant victory. ... Praise be to Allah, the Lord of the worlds. [24]

In 1307, Ala-uddin's army made another foray across the mountains to Devgiri, after Ramadev's son, Singhana, refused to pay the annual tribute. Ramadev, by informing on his son, assured his own favor with the Sultanate and was treated as a loyal Muslim ally until his death in 1311. In 1313, when once again Singhana refused to pay tribute to the Sultan, he was tortured and slain by the Sultan's armies. After that, Devgiri became Daulatabad, a base for Khalji military operations in the Deccan and the far south.

In 1316, Ala-uddin, having ruined his health owing to intemperance and excess, had to take to his bed. Suffering from paranoid delusions, he accused his own family of a plot against him, and had his wife and two sons imprisoned and several of his loyal officers put to death. His grief and rage only tended to increase his disorder, and, on the evening of December 16, 1316, he died.

In the history books of this world, the list of ambitious warlords and their murderous exploits is endless. Ala-uddin merely added one more infamous name to that pitiable list, and then faded from the memory of mankind; while his contemporary, Jnaneshvar, though little known outside his own small circle of friends, and all but ignored by historians, became immortal. In the unrecorded history book of divine souls, the name of Jnaneshvar will forever remain, written large among the greatest and most beloved of God.

* * *

NOTES

1. Quran, IX, 5,6.

2. Quran, VIII, 39-40.

3. Elliott & Dawson, p. 179 ff.

4. Rawlinson, p. 224.

5. *dinars*: silver coins.

6. *miskals*: measure of weight approximate to the pound.

7. Majumdar, *The Struggle For Empire*, p. 14.

8. Majumdar, *The Struggle For Empire;* from the Foreword by K.M. Munshi, p. xi-xii.

9. Srivastava, *Medieval Indian Culture*, p. 42.

10. Nizami, p. 116.

11. Nizami, p. 103.

12. Jnaneshvar, *Jnaneshvari*, Chapter 18, verse 1783; volume II, p. 350.

13. Elliott & Dawson, p. 179 ff.

14. Ferishta, p. 158.

15. Ferishta, p. 167.

16. Namadev, *abhanga* included in the *Adi Granth* of the Sikhs.

17. Adapted from the narrative of Gangadevi, the female consort of prince Kampana of Vijaya-nagara, written during the Mulsim conquest of Madura; from Majumdar, *The Delhi Sultanate*, p. 631.

18. Adapted from the narrative of Isana Nagara, written during the reign of Ala-uddin Husain Shah (1493-1514); from Majumdar, *The Delhi Sultanate,* p. 633.

19. Adapted from the eye-witness account of the African Muslim traveller, Ibn Batutah (1304-1378), from his *Rehla* ("Travels"); quoted by Majumdar, *The Delhi Sultanate,* p. 463, note 90a.

20. *maund*: 28.25 pounds. Fifty *maunds*: 1,412½ lbs.

21. Ferishta, p. 173.

22. Ferishta, p. 176.

23. Elliott & Dawson, p. 179 ff.

24. Majumdar, *The Delhi Sultanate,* pp. 625-626.

BIBLIOGRAPHY

Abbott, Justin, *The Poet Saints Of Maharashtra,* United Theological College, Poona, 1926.

Bahirat, B.P., *The Philosophy Of Jnanadeva,* Pandharpur Research Society, 1956.

de Barry, Wm. T., (ed.) *Sources Of Indian Tradition,* Columbia University Press, New York, 1958.

Elliott, H.M. and Dowson, J., *The History Of India As Told By Its Own Historians,* Vol. II., 1867-77.

Ferishta, Mahomed Kasim, *History Of The Rise Of The Mahomedan Power In India* (translated from the original Persian by John Briggs); Vol. I, Editions Indian, Calcutta, 1829, 1966.

Husain, Agha Mahdi (ed.), *Rutuhu's Salatin or Shah Namah-i-Hind Of Isami,* Vol. I, Asia Publishing House, New York, 1967.

Jnaneshvar, *Jnaneshvari* (translated by V.G. Pradhan and edited by H.M. Lambert), 2 Vols., Allen & Unwin, London, 1967.

Keshavadas, Sadguru Sant, *Lord Panduranga And His Minstrels,* Bharattiya Vidya Bhuvan, Bombay, 1977.

Kincaid, C.A. and Parasnis, R.B., *A History Of The Maratha People,* S. Chand & Co., New Delhi, 1968.

Lal, K.S., *History Of The Khaljis (A.D. 1290-1320),* Asia Publishing House, New York, 1967.

Majumdar, R.C. (ed.), *The Delhi Sultanate, Vol. VI in The History And Culture Of The Indian People,* Bharatiya Vidya Bhavan, Bombay, 1960.

_______, *The Struggle For Empire, Vol. V in The History And Culture Of The Indian People*, Bharatiya Vidya Bhavan, Bombay, 1957.

Nizami, Khaliq Ahmad, *Some Aspects Of Religion And Politics In India During The Thirteenth Century,* Asia Publishing House, Bombay, 1961.

Ranade, R.D., *Mysticism In Maharashtra, Vol. VII of The History Of Indian Philosophy,* Belvalkar and Ranade, Aryabhushan Press, Poona, 1933; reprinted as *Mysticism In India* by State University of New York, New York, 1983.

Rawlinson, H.G., *India: A Short Cultural History,* The Grosset Press, London, 1937.
Srivastava, A.L., *Medieval Indian Culture,* Agarwala & Co., Agra, 1964.
______, *The History Of India (1000 A.D. - 1707 A.D.),* Agarwala & Co. Ltd., Agra, 1964.

BOOK TWO:

The Works of Jnaneshvar

PREFACE TO BOOK TWO: The Works Of Jnaneshvar

Jnaneshvar was a revolutionary, a pioneer, in the expression of mystical truths in the Marathi language. Prior to him, all such literature had been framed in the classical Sanskrit; and Marathi, the popular language of Maharashtra, had been regarded as unfit for the transmission of sacred knowledge. Jnaneshvar changed all that. And today, the people of Maharashtra honor Jnaneshvar as their greatest poet-saint; millions visit his tomb at Alandi each year, and his songs are still sung daily in temples throughout the land. The reason that he is so revered and beloved in his own land becomes easily understood when we discover the poetic works of Jnaneshvar. Even in English translation, the profundity of his thought, the rich profusity of his imagery, and the unmistakeable style of his homespun wisdom, not to mention his tender age, distinguish his works as those of a unique genius.

If we insist on tracing the major influences in Jnaneshvar's development, we must acknowledge first of all India's great legacy of scriptures and philosophical treatises. Long before the time of Jnaneshvar, an ancient and exquisite literature existed, testifying to the mystical experience of the Self. Jnaneshvar was familiar with much of this literature; he knew the philosophical works such as the *Upanishads*, Shankara's *Vivekachudamani*, the *Shiva Sutras* of Vasugupta, and many other ancient and contemporary commentaries by both Vaishnavite and Shaivite authors. He was especially fond of the literature of devotional mysticism, such as the *Bhagavad Gita* and the *Shrimad Bhagavatam*; and was expertly familiar with the popular epics, the *Ramayana* and the *Mahabharata*.

There was also the influence of his brother and Guru, Nivritti. Nivritti passed on to Jnaneshvar the yogic secrets which had been taught him by Gahininath, a Guru of the Nath lineage. Essential to the tradition of the Naths is the necessity of having a living Guru who is able to impart, not only verbalized knowledge, but the very state of Self-realization to his disciple. The direct experience of the Self was said to be transmitted on the subtle level by the voluntary grace of a Master who was capable of instilling his own consciousness and energy into the disciple. Jnaneshvar was convinced by his own experience that Gahini had passed this supramental knowledge to Nivritti, and that Nivritti had passed it on to him.

It is worthwhile to note also that, during Jnaneshvar's time and in his own region of Maharashtra, a popular mystical movement was already active and influential; it was the movement called Mahanubhava, which means, "the great [mystical] experience." The Mahanubhavas were a group of mystics who placed great emphasis on the need to obtain this "great experience" in order to truly comprehend the nature of man and reality. The movement seems to have been started in 1263 by a Swami Chakradhara who died around the time of Jnaneshvar's birth. Its members eschewed idol-worship and allowed the initiation into the Order of *sannyasa* (monkhood) not only to brahmins, as was the traditional practice, but to men of all castes and sects.

Some of the ideals and tenets of this sect were contained in the *Chakradhara-Siddhanta-Sutras* of Keshobhasa, written around 1280, the *Lilacharita* of Mhaimbhata (1288), and the *Rukminisvayamvara* of Narendra (1292). A woman poetess of this sect, Mahadaisa, wrote her *Dhavale*, a collection of devotional songs, around 1287. Clearly, the Mahanubhavas were very active around the time and place of Jnaneshvar's creative years, and though he is not thought to have been in any way connected with them, the very title of his spiritual masterpiece, *Amritanubhav*, seems an obvious reference to them.

Jnaneshvar's two major literary works are *Jnaneshvari*, a lengthy work based on the *Bhagavad Gita,* and *Amritanubhav* ("The Nectar Of Mystical Experience"). In the West, Jnaneshvar is justly famous for his *Jnaneshvari*, but his other works have received little attention or recognition here. In the present selection of his works, we have not included excerpts from *Jnaneshvari,* as that work has already been adequately presented in the excellent translation by V.G. Pradhan. We have included here, however, his second major work, *Amritanubhav,* in its entirety.

Amritanubhav was written immediately after *Jnan-*

eshvari, and is Jnaneshvar's free-style expression of the knowledge of the Self which he himself had obtained to the fullest degree. *Jnaneshvari*, based as it was on the *Bhagavad Gita*, followed a pre-established format; but in *Amritanubhav*, Jnaneshvar was able to follow his own chain of thought without the encumbrance of scriptural pre-conceptions.

In addition to *Amritanubhav*, included here in translation for the first time, are *Haripatha* ("Sing The Name Of Hari"), a collection of devotional songs focusing on the value of chanting the name of God; and *Changadev Pasashti*, ("Letter To Changadev") which Jnaneshvar wrote to a fellow Yogi as a presentation of the essence of his spiritual teachings.

AMRITANUBHAV

AMRITANUBHAV

THE NECTAR OF MYSTICAL EXPERIENCE

Chapter One: Introductory Note

It is only as a means of categorization that we may speak of Amritanubhav *as a 'philosophic' work, for Jnaneshvar was no philosopher, in the ordinary sense of the word; what he wrote was no mere speculation or theory, but was an attempt to explain what he had experienced first-hand in the mystical experience of Unity. In that mystical experience, the individual's mind experiences itself as the universal Consciousness from which the entire universe is projected. It is an eternal and unlimited Consciousness which underlies all phenomenal existence, and yet which is Itself entirely devoid of phenomena, being the Source and Producer of all perceivable phenomena.*

*It is the paradoxicality of this experience which prevents it from being explicable in the terminology of conventional logic. For the mystic not only experiences himself as the one pure and unblemished Mind; he experiences, at the same time, the manifestation and de-manifestation of all cosmic phenomena within himself. It is unquestionably a Unity, just as an individual mind and its thoughts are a unity, but there are these two aspects to It: one, the eternal and unlimited Consciousness, and the other, the projected thought-image which is the universe. In Western philosophical terminology, these two are referred to as God (*Theos*) and His Word (*Logos*); in India, they are called "Brahman" and Its "Maya," "Purusha" and Its "Prakrti," or "Shiva" and Its "Shakti," depending on one's preference.*

Jnaneshvar, in his earlier work, Jnaneshvari, *which is a poetic reiteration of the philosophy of the* Bhagavad Gita, *adhered to the terms for these two complements most commonly used in the Gita, namely, "Brahman"-"Maya" or "Purusha"-"Prakrti". But when it came to writing* Amritanubhav, *his own free expression of his own mystical experience, he resorted to the terminology common to the Shaivite philosophical tradition, and used the terms, "Shiva" and "Shakti." These two, Shiva and Shakti, form a unique relationship to one another; they are at the same time distinguishable from, and yet identical to, one another. They are conceptually and categorically two, and yet they are ultimately a unit. Shakti is the perceivable aspect of Shiva. Shiva is the invisible substratum of Shakti. Like the ocean and its waves, they are indivisibly one.*

In his opening chapter of Amritanubhav, Jnaneshvar refers to these two principles as "the god" and "the goddess." In this way, he describes in metaphorical fashion their relationship as an inseparable husband and wife, acknowledging their apparent duality, while continually hearking back to their essential unity. He recognized the necessity, if one was to speak at all of their ultimate unity, to acknowledge these two complementary aspects of the One, and to distinguish between them according to their characteristics. Yet, to Jnaneshvar, who had obtained the "vision" of Truth, everything before his eyes was simply the delightful sport of God; to him, nothing else existed but God, and all talk of duality was misleading. As he says, "It is because of the union of these two [Shiva and Shakti] that the whole universe exists. [Yet] their duality disappears when their essential unity is seen."

This, the opening chapter of Amritanubhav, *is undoubtedly one of the most strikingly beautiful poetic expressions of this duality-in-unity ever written. In it, Jnaneshvar, the poet, portrays, with symbol and metaphor, that mystery which remains forever inexpressible in the language of philosophy and logic.*

CHAPTER ONE

Invocation

I take refuge in the God
Who is revealed in the person of
The glorious Nivrittinath. [1]
He is the one indescribable Bliss
Who is unborn, immortal, and ever-unchanged.

I honor the divine Wisdom
In the form of the Guru,
Who, overflowing with compassion,
Showers his blessings on all,
And whose commands point the way to victory.

Though one, He appears as Shiva and Shakti.
Whether it is Shiva joined to Shakti
Or Shakti joined to Shiva,
No one can tell.

I bow to these parents of the worlds,
Who, by revealing to each other their oneness,
Enable me also to know it.

I make obeisance to Shambhu (Shiva),
That perfect Lord who is
The Cause of the beginning,
Preservation, and end of the world;
The Manifestation of the beginning,
Middle and end of the world;
And the Dissolution of the three as well.

The Union Of Shiva And Shakti

1. I offer obeisance to the God and Goddess,
The limitless primal parents of the universe.

2. The lover, out of boundless love,
Has become the Beloved.
Both are made of the same substance
And share the same food.

3. Out of love for each other, they merge;
And again, they separate for the pleasure of being two.

4. They are not entirely the same,
Nor are they not the same.
We cannot say exactly what they are.

5. Their one great desire is to enjoy each other;
Yet they never allow their unity to be disturbed,
Even as a joke.

6. They are so averse to separation
That even their child, the universe,
Does not disturb their union.

7. Though they perceive the universe
Of inanimate and animate creation
Emanating from themselves,
They do not recognize a third.

8. They sit together on the same ground,
Wearing the same garment of light.
From time past remembrance they have lived thus,
United in Bliss.

9. Difference itself merged in their sweet union
When, seeing their intimacy,
It could find no duality to enjoy.

10. Because of God, the Goddess exists;
And without Her, He is not.
They exist only because of each other.

11. How sweet is their union!
The whole world is too small to contain them,
Yet they live happily in the smallest particle.

12. They regard each other as their own Self,
And neither creates so much as a blade
Of grass without the other.

13. These two are the only ones
Who dwell in this home called the universe.
When the Master of the house sleeps,
The Mistress stays awake,
And performs the functions of both.

14. When He awakes, the whole house disappears,
And nothing at all is left.

15. They became two for the purpose of diversity;
And both are seeking each other
For the purpose of becoming one.

16. Each is an object to the other,
And both are subjects to each other.
Only when together do they enjoy happiness.

17. It is Shiva alone who lives in all forms;
He is both the male and the female.
It is because of the union of these two complements
That the whole universe exists.

18. Two lutes: one note.
Two flowers: one fragrance.
Two lamps: one light.

19. Two lips: one word.
Two eyes: one sight.
These two: one universe.

20. Though manifesting duality,
These two -- the eternal Pair --
Are eating from the same dish.

21. The Shakti, endowed with chastity and fidelity,
Cannot live without Her Lord;
And without Her,
The Doer-of-all cannot appear.

22. Since He appears because of Her,
And She exists because of Her Lord,
The two cannot be distinguished at all.

23. Sugar and its sweetness
Cannot be separated from one another,
Nor can camphor and its fragrance.

24. If there are flames,
There is also fire.
If we catch hold of Shakti,
We have Shiva as well.

25. The Sun appears to shine because of its rays,
But it is the Sun itself which produces the rays.
In fact, that glorious Sun and its shining
Are one and the same.

26. To have a reflection, one must have an object;
If we see a reflection, then we infer that
An object exists.
Likewise, the supreme Reality, which is one,
Appears to be two.

27. Through Her,
The absolute Void becomes the manifest world;
But Her existence
Is derived from Her Lord.

28. Shiva Himself became His beloved;
But without Her presence,
No universe exists.

29. Because of Her form,
God is seen as the world;
But He created Her form
Of Himself.

30. Embarrassed by Her formless Husband
And Her own graceful form,
She adorned Him with a universe
Of myriad names and forms.

31. In unity, there is little to behold;
So She, the mother of abundance,
Brought forth the world as a play.

32. She made evident the glory of Her Lord
By spreading out Her own body-form.
And He made Her famous by concealing Himself.

33. He takes the role of Witness
Out of love of watching Her.
But when Her appearance is withdrawn,
The role of Witness is abandoned as well.

34. Through Her,
He assumes the form of the universe;
Without Her,
He is left naked.

35. Although He is manifest,
He Himself cannot be seen.
It is only because of Her
That He appears as universal form.

36. When He is awakened by Her,
Shiva perceives the world.
Then He enjoys this dish She serves,
As well as She who serves.

37. While He sleeps, She gives birth
To the animate and inanimate worlds.
When She rests,
Her Husband disappears.

38. When He conceals Himself,
He cannot be discovered without Her grace.
They are as mirrors, each to the other.

39. When He embraces Her,
It is His own bliss that Shiva enjoys.
He is the enjoyer of everything,
But there is no enjoyment without Her.

40. She is His form,
But Her beauty comes from Him.
By their intermingling,
They are, together, enjoying this feast.

41. Shiva and Shakti are the same,
Like air and its motion,
Or gold and its lustre.

42. Fragrance cannot be separated from musk,
Nor heat from fire;
Neither can Shakti be separated from Shiva.

43. If night and day were to approach the Sun,
Both would disappear.
In the same way, *their* duality would vanish
If their essential Unity were seen.

44. In fact, [the duality of] Shiva and Shakti
Cannot exist in that primal unitive state
From which AUM emanates.

45. Jnanadev says,
"I honor the primal pair of Shiva and Shakti
Who, by swallowing up the sweet dish
of name and form,
Reveal their underlying Unity."

46. Embracing each other, they merge into one,
As darkness merges into light
At the breaking of dawn.

47. All levels of speech, from *Para* to *Vaikari,* [1]
Merge into silence
When their true nature is realized,
Just as the ocean and the Ganges both merge
Into the primal waters
When the universal Deluge comes.

48. Then, the air along with its motion merges
Into the universal air;
The Sun along with its brilliance merges
Into the elemental fire at that time.

49. Likewise, while attempting
To see Shiva and Shakti,
Both the seer and his vision disappear.
Again and again I offer salutations
To that universal pair.

50. They are like a stream of knowledge
From which a knower cannot drink
Unless he gives up himself.

51. When such is the case,
If I remain separate in order to honor them,
It is only a pretended separation.

52. My homage is like that
Of a golden ornament
Worshipping gold.

53. When my tongue says the word, "tongue,"
Is there any difference between the
Organ which utters the word
And the object signified by that word?

54. Although the names, "Ganges" and "ocean" are different,
When they commingle,
Are their waters not the same?

55. The Sun is both the source
And the object of illumination;
Still it is only one.

56. If moonlight illumines the moon,
Of if a lamp is revealed by the light of itself,
Is there any separation here?

57. When the lustre of a pearl
Plays upon itself,
It only enhances itself.

58. Is the sound of AUM divided into three
Simply because it contains three letters?
Or is the letter 'N' divided into three
Because of the three lines by which it is formed?

59. So long as Unity is undisturbed,
And a graceful pleasure is thereby derived,
Why should not the water find delight
In the floral fragrance of its own rippled surface?

60. It is in this manner I bow
To the inseparable Shiva and Shakti.

61. A reflected image vanishes
When the mirror is taken away.
The ripples on the water vanish
When the wind becomes still.

62. A man returns to himself
When he awakens from sleep;
Likewise, I have perceived the God and Goddess
By waking from my ego.

63. When salt dissolves,
It becomes one with the ocean;
When my ego dissolved,
I became one with Shiva and Shakti.

64. I have paid homage to Shiva and Shakti
By uniting with them --
Just as, when the outer covering
Of the hollow banyan tree is removed,
The inner space becomes united with the outer. [2]

Chapter Two: Introductory Note

Jnaneshvar had experienced the "vision of unity," had realized the Self of the universe; and he attributed this attainment to the initiating and nourishing grace of his brother, Nivritti. Jnaneshvar's relationship to his brother was a unique one, for Nivritti was also his revered Guru. A fraternal relationship is a very special one, no doubt, but the relationship between a disciple and his Guru is one of utter, uncompromising, devotion. Jnaneshvar felt this kind of devotion to Nivritti, and looked on him as the very manifestation of God, a living form of the one formless Reality in whom resided the power of grace.

In the Nath tradition handed on to Nivritti from his own Guru, Gahininath, and in the Hindu tradition generally, the Guru holds a very significant place. Through his own Self-realization, the Master is said to obtain the power of transmitting his own elevated awareness to his disciples, through his touch, or glance, or simply by the power of his will. Even the words of the Guru have the power to profoundly affect the soul of the disciple. We can readily experience this elevating influence of the word as we read and absorb the words of Jnaneshvar, who, in this work, serves as Guru to the reader.

Such transmission of Self-awareness is called, in the Shaivite tradition, "Shaktipat." It is said to awaken in the disciple the latent Intelligence which, evolving in the disciple, leads him to Self-realization. This evolutionary potential is said to reside in a latent, or unevolved, state in all human beings in the subtle nerve-channel at the base of the spine. And when it is stimulated into activity, or wakefulnes, by the Guru, this evolutionary energy, known as Kundalini Shakti *("the coiled energy"), begins its evolutionary ascent, rising through several different stages of awareness, corresponding to the ascending stages along the spinal column. When this intelligent energy reaches its full development, corresponding to its ascent to the top of the head, the disciple experiences the union of Shakti with Shiva; i.e., realizes his oneness with God.*

The true Guru, who possesses this power, is therefore thought of by his disciple as "the dispeller of darkness," "the grace-bestowing power of God." It is in this manner that Jnaneshvar regarded Nivritti, most sincerely and unreservedly, as synonymous with Shiva; and in this, the second chapter of Amritanubhav, *Jnandev offers his fervent paean of praise to the Guru, worshipping him as the very embodiment of God.*

CHAPTER TWO

Salutations To Sri Nivritti

1. Now I offer salutations to him
Who is the well-spring of the garden of sadhana
The auspicious conduit of divine Will,
And, though formless,
The very incarnation of compassion.

2. I offer salutations to him
Who comes to the aid of the Self
Which is suffering limitation
In the wilderness of ignorance.

3. I bow to my Guru, Nivritti,
Who, by slaying the elephant of Maya,
Has made a dish of the pearls
Taken from its temple.

4. By his mere glance,
Bondage becomes liberation,
And the knower becomes the known.

5. He distributes the gold of liberation to all,
Both the great and the small;
It is He who gives the vision of the Self.

6. As for his powers,
He surpasses even the greatness of Shiva.
He is a mirror in which the Self
Sees the reflection of its own bliss.

7. It is by his grace
That all the moon-phases of sadhana
Culminate in the full moon of realization.

8. All the sadhaka's efforts cease
When he meets the Guru.
He is the ocean in which the river
Of activity has ceased to be.

9. When he is absent,
One wears the lovely cloak of appearance;
When he appears,
The cloak of diversity vanishes.

10. The Sun of his grace turns the darkness of ignorance
Into the light of Self-knowledge.

11. The water of his grace
Washes the soul so clean
That he regards even Shiva as unclean,
And does not wish to be touched
Even by him.

12. He abandoned the greatness of his own state
To save his disciple,
Yet his true greatness has never been abandoned.

13. Alone, there is no happiness.
Therefore, the pure Consciousness
Assumes the forms of Guru and disciple.

14. By just a little sprinkle of his grace,
The poison of ignorance is changed into nectar --
The nectar of limitless knowledge.

15. When knowledge discovers him within,
He swallows up the knower;
And still he does not become impure.

16. With his help,
The soul attains the state of Brahman;
But if he is indifferent,
Brahman has no more worth than a blade of grass.

17. Those who faithfully endeavor,
Regarding his will as law,
Obtain the ripe fruit of their efforts.

18. Unless the well-spring of his glance
Waters the garden of knowledge,
There will be no fruit in the hand.

19. By casting a mere glance,
He makes the world of appearance
Recede and vanish.
Though his conquest is great,
He does not call it his own.

20. He has attained the great status of Guru
By possessing no status.
His wealth is his ability
To rid us of what does not exist.

21. He is the rock of refuge
Which saves us from drowning
In the sea which does not exist.
Those who are saved are
Released from time and space.

22. He is the calm and ever-perfect sky within.
To that, the outer sky cannot compare.

23. From his light,
The moon with her cool beams is made;
The Sun derives its brilliance
From a single ray of his light.

24. He is like an astrologer whom Shiva,
Weary of assuming individual forms,
Has commissioned to find an auspicious time
For the regaining of his own state.

25. He is like the moon whose form
Is not diminished, but enhanced,
By the wearing of a gown of light.

26. Though present, he is not seen.
Though he is light, he does not illumine.
Though he always is, he is not in any place.

27. How much more shall I say,
Using the words, "he" and "who"?
He cannot be explained by words.

28. He is indescribable.
In his unity, where there is no duality,
Words become silent.

29. The object of knowledge reveals itself
When the means of knowledge ceases to be.
It is this non-being which he loves the most.

30. Though we may wish to have a glimpse of him,
Even that seeing, in his kingdom,
Is a stain.

31. When such is the case,
How could one find entrance to his kingdom
By means of praise or by reference to him?
Even his name becomes merged in him!

32. The Self does not seek himself;
Neither does he conceal himself from himself.
He merely retains a name
To serve as a veil.

33. How can he destroy what does not exist?
How can he be called "the Destroyer"?

34. The Sun is called the destroyer of darkness,
But when did the Sun perceive any darkness?

35. That which is illusory becomes real,
That which is inanimate becomes animate,
And that which is impossible becomes possible,
All through his marvellous sport.

36. Through your wondrous power, you create illusions;
And then you reject them as mere illusions.
You remain beyond the illusions;
You are not the object of any kind of vision.

37. O Satguru, you are so mysterious!
How then am I to treat of you?
You do not allow yourself to be defined by words.

38. You have created so many names and forms,
And destroyed them again through your power,
Yet still you are not satisfied.

39. You do not give your friendship to anyone
Without taking away his sense of individuality.

40. If one tries to attach a name to him,
Even the name, "Self," does not fit.
He refuses to be confined to a particular thing.

41. To the Sun, there is no night;
To pure water, there is no salt;
To one who is awake, there is no sleep.

42. In the presence of fire, camphor cannot remain;
In his presence, name and form cease to be.

43. Though I try to bow to him,
He does not remain before me
As an object of my worship.
He does not allow any sense of difference.

44. The Sun does not become something else
In order to serve as a means for its rising;
Neither does he become an object for my worship.

45. By no means may one place oneself before him;
He has removed the possibility
Of his being an object of anyone's worship.

46. If you mirror the sky,
No reflection may be seen;
Neither is he an object
Which someone may worship.

47. So what if he is not an object of worship!
Why should it seem so mysterious to me?
But he does not leave any trace
Of the one who goes to worship!

48. When the outside of a garment is opened,
The inside is opened as well.

49. Or, as a mirrored image must vanish
When the object of reflection is gone,
So must the one who worships vanish
When the object of worship disappears.

50. Our vision is worthless where there is no form.
We are placed in such a state
By the grace of his feet.

51. The flame of a lamp is kept burning continually
By the combination of the wick and the oil;
A piece of camphor cannot keep it burning.

52. For as soon as the camphor and flame are united,
Both of them vanish at once.

53. When he is seen,
Both worshipper and the object of worship vanish
As dreams vanish at the moment of waking.

54. By these verses I have made a finish of duality,
And also honored my beloved Sri Guru.

55. How wonderful is his friendship!
He has manifested duality
In the form of Guru and disciple
Where there is not even a place for one!

56. How does he have a close relationship with himself
When there is no one other than himself?
He can never become anything other than himself!

57. He becomes as vast as the sky,
Including the entire universe within himself.
Within him
Even darkness and non-existence dwell.

58. An ocean fulfills the needs of all,
Yet it cannot be fulfilled itself.
Also in the Guru's house
Such contradictions happily live together.

59. There is no intimacy between night and day,
But they are one in the eyes of the Sun.

60. Although the supreme Reality is one,
Differences arise within It.
How does differentiation detract
From the unity of the Whole?
Does the existence of opposites within
Contradict the unity of the Whole?

61. The words, "Guru" and "disciple"
Refer to but one;
The Guru alone exists as both these forms.

62. Both in gold and in golden ornaments,
There is nothing but gold.
In the moon and in moonlight
There is nothing but the moon.

63. Camphor and its fragrance are nothing but camphor;
Sugar and its sweetness are nothing but sugar.

64. Although the Guru and disciple appear to be two,
It is the Guru alone who masquerades as both.

65. When you look in a mirror and see your own face,
You know that both are only yourself.

66. If a person awakes in a solitary place
When no one else is about,
Then one may be sure that he is both
The awakened and the awakener as well.

67. Just as the awakened and the awakener are the same,
The Guru is both the receiver of knowledge
And the one who imparts it as well.
Still, he continues to uphold the relationship
Of Master and disciple.

68. If one could see his own eye without a mirror,
There would be no need of this sport of the Guru.

69. Therefore, he nourishes this intimate relationship
Without causing duality or disturbing the Unity.

70. His name is Nivritti.
Nivritti is his splendor.
Nivritti is the glory of his kingdom.

71. He is not the 'nivritti'
Which means the absence of activity:

72. That 'nivritti' is the product
Of 'pravritti', or activity --
Just as night is necessitated
By its opposite, day.
He is not that 'nivritti'.

73. He is the pure and supreme Lord;
He is not the kind of jewel
Which needs something else
To cause it to sparkle.

74. The moon spreads her soft light,
Pervading the entire sky.
It is she herself
Who enhances her own form.

75. Likewise, Nivritti is the cause of Nivritti.
He is like a flower become a nose
In order to enjoy its own fragrance.

76. Would a mirror be needed
If one's vision were able to turn back on itself
And perceive the fairness of one's own complexion?

77. Though night dissolves and daylight comes,
Is not the Sun unchanged,
Without the need to make an effort
To return to himself?

78. Nivritti is not an object of knowledge
Which requires various proofs
To show that it exists;
There is no doubt that he is the Guru.

79. Salutations to the holy feet of the Guru
Whose actionlessness is absolute,
Without any trace of activity.

80. Jnanadeva says, "This salutation to Sri Guru
Satisfies the requirements
Of all the four levels of speech."

Chapter Three: Introductory Note

In the Third Chapter, Jnaneshvar attempts to expose the error of confusing relative knowledge with the absolute Knowledge, which is synonymous with the Self. When the Self is experienced, It shines forth as all-comprehensive Knowledge, a Knowledge in which there is no separation between the knower and what is known. It is this absolute Knowledge which exists eternally as the Self at the subtlest core of our being. Relative knowledge, however, is the product of thought; and thought is anterior to that absolute state, representing a leap from the unitive awareness of the Self to a separative awareness, wherein the thinker becomes distinct from the object of his thought, and becomes a separate and distinct entity in a world of multiple entities.

In the Shaivite philosophical tradition, the subtlest level at which thought emanates from that perfect Knowledge is called Para, *corresponding to the subtlest body of man, the supra-causal body. This is where all thought-impulses begin. At a less subtle level, called* pashyanti, *which corresponds to the causal body, the the thought takes form. And at the level called* madhyama, *corresponding to the subtle body, the thought is fully formulated and may be heard within. This thought is then uttered at the gross level, called* vaikari, *and emitted as speech. These are the four levels of speech; they are the consecutive degrees of expression of relative, or dualistic, knowledge. But this knowledge is not the absolute Knowledge; it is but a pale and dim reflection.*

When the enlightenment experience, the revelation of the Self, wanes and passes, what remains is a memory, an intellectually formulable expression of that absolute Knowledge, but it is not that Knowledge. The Self may be formulated in thought and speech, but that knowledge is not the absolute Knowledge; for thought and speech occur only anterior to the breakdown of unity into subject and object, and arise only under those conditions. The attempt to describe the Self, therefore, is like the attempt to draw a picture of the water's calm surface by stirring in the water with a stick. Or like trying to express silence with a brass band.

As Jnaneshvar acknowledges, it is thought which

brings the awareness to that degree of subtlety where it can experience itself as pure Knowledge where all intellectualizing is transcended; but the difference between that pure Knowledge and mere intellectual knowledge is one not merely of degree, but of kind. Relative knowledge, Jnaneshvar rightly points out, is dependent upon its counterpart, ignorance, for existence; they are interdependent, and exist only relative to one another. Whereas absolute Knowledge exists eternally, is independent of these two relative, opposing, states, and has no opposite, being all-inclusive.

In that pure, absolute Knowledge, there is no longer a separation between the knower and what is known. The knower knows himself to be all. He no longer thinks 'about' a something; he is the thinker, the thought, the object of thought, on an infinite cosmic scale. In the aftermath of that experience, he may regard himself as "liberated," free; for he retains a knowledge of that Knowledge, which utterly transforms his way of looking at himself and the world. But, as Jnaneshvar points out, this knowledge, this 'freedom' is not the real Knowledge and Freedom, which exists in Itself, beyond the duality of knower and known.

CHAPTER THREE

The Requirements Of Speech

1. It is the calling aloud of these four levels of speech
Which awakens the Self.
But even this waking is a kind of sleep.

2. It is true that these four levels of speech
Are conducive to soul-liberation,
But with the destruction of ignorance,
These also are destroyed.

3. Just as hands and feet depart along with the body
At the time of death,

Or as the subtle senses depart along with the mind,
Or as the Sun's rays depart with the setting Sun,

4. Or as dreams depart when sleep comes to an end,
So the four levels of speech depart
Along with ignorance.

5. When iron is burned, it continues to exist as liquid;
Fuel burnt continues as fire.

6. Salt dissolved in water
Continues to exist as taste;
Sleep dispelled continues as wakefulness.

7. In the same way, although the four levels of speech
Are destroyed along with ignorance,
They continue to live as knowledge of Reality.

8. It's true, they light the lamp of knowledge
Through their sacrifice,
But this kind of knowledge is a futile exertion.

9. Sleep, while it remains,
Is the cause of one's dreams;
And when it vanishes,
It is the cause of one's becoming awake.
It is sleep that is the cause of both.

10. In the same way,
Ignorance, while it remains,
Is the cause of false knowledge;
And when it vanishes,
Is the cause of true knowledge.

11. But, living or dead,
This ignorance entangles the individual
By binding him
With either slavery or a false sense of freedom.

12. If freedom itself is a kind of bondage,
Why should the word, "freedom," be given to it?

13. A child is satisfied
By the death of an ogre in a dream;
But it does not even exist for others!
How should they be affected by its death?

14. If someone bewails
The loss of a broken vase which never existed,
Would we consider that person wise?

15. If bondage itself is unreal,
How can freedom arise from its destruction?
This freedom is only something created
By the self-destruction of ignorance.

16. Sadashiva,
In the *Shiva Sutras,*
Has declared that knowledge itself is bondage. [1]

17. It is not that we accept this
Merely because it was said by Shiva or by
Krishna.
It can be understood
Even if they had not said it.

18. Sri Krishna (in the *Bhagavad Gita*)
Has elaborately explained how
The quality of *sattva* binds one
With the cords of knowledge. [2]

19. If the Self, which is pure Knowledge itself,
Requires the help of another knowledge,
Would that not be like the Sun seeking help
Of another light?

20. It is meaningless to say
That the Self is itself Knowledge
If Its greatness depends
On some knowledge other than Itself.
If a lamp desires another lamp
To give it light,
It must be that it has gone out.

21. Could one who was ignorant of his own existence
Wander about to various countries in search of himself?

22. How might one declare
That he was happy to remember himself
After so many days?

23. Also, if the Self,
Who is himself pure Consciousness,
Thinks, "I am conscious of myself -- I am He!"
Such knowledge would be bondage.

24. This kind of knowledge is deplorable,
Since it conceals the original Knowledge
And fosters the illusion of freedom.

25. Therefore,
When the ego of the individual is destroyed,
And ignorance vanishes,
The four levels of speech --
Which are ornaments of the four bodies --
Also vanish.

26. When ignorance, being utterly dejected,
Enters the fire of Consciousness
Along with her organs,
Nothing remains but the ashes of knowledge.

27. When camphor is dissolved in water,
It cannot be seen,
But can be detected as fragrance in the water.

28. When ashes are smeared on the body,
The loose particles may fall away,
But the white coloration remains.

29. Even though the water of a river
May have ceased to flow,
Still it remains as moisture in the soil.

30. Though one's shadow may not be seen at noon-time,
Still it remains under one's feet.

31. So, also, the Knowledge
That swallows everything other than Itself
Is merged in the ultimate Reality,
But remains as knowledge.

32. The requirements of the four levels of speech
Cannot be satisfied even by their self-sacrifice.
I have satisfied them by bowing my head
At the holy feet of the Guru.

33. When the four levels of speech are destroyed,
They remain as that knowledge
Which is itself a kind of ignorance.

Chapter Four: Introductory Note

Chapter Four is a continuation on the same theme. The understanding of the nature of reality which arises through discursive thought dispels ignorance, says Jnaneshvar, but that knowledge is, itself, an illusory knowledge compared to the Knowledge which is synonymous with the absolute Self. The knowledge consisting of logical reasonings and proofs may produce intellectual understanding, but that is merely the other side of the coin of ignorance; such word-knowledge can never produce Knowledge; i.e., the revelation of the Self.

In this respect, Amritanubhav *is reminiscent of the writings of some Western seers, like Heraclitus, and particularly Nicholas of Cusa (1401-1464), who asserted in his book,* On Learned Ignorance, *that no amount of intellectual knowledge (which he called "learned ignorance") was capable of revealing the Absolute. Like Nicholas, Jnaneshvar takes great pains to explain that, when the absolute Unity is experienced in the mystical "vision," all relative knowledge is swallowed up along with ignorance, and only that pure all-encompassing Awareness remains. What had previously been mere 'understanding' expands to the degree that it transcends itself in a sudden dawning of direct* Knowing, *beyond the intermediary of the intellect, at once dissolving the distinction between knower and known.*

It would appear that, in discrediting intellectual knowledge, Jnaneshvar is, ironically, establishing the futility of his own dissertation; but this is not so. Jnaneshvar acknowledges the usefulness of intellectual understanding, i.e., relative knowledge, as a preparation for Self-realization. He compares such understanding to the awakening from sleep which is, itself, abandoned to the steady state of wakefulness, or to the flame produced by burning camphor, which is, itself, extinguished simultaneous with the annihilation of the camphor. While, in these two analogies, the awakening and the flame are extinguished in the end, both are necessary and essential ingredients in the accomplishment of that end. In the same way, though knowledge is extinguished in the realization of the Self, it is necessary to the attainment of that end.

Jnaneshvar goes on to explain the paradoxical

nature of that pure Knowledge, whose utterly unique status precludes any accurate comparisons or analogies. It IS, yet it is a "nothing," says Jnaneshvar; It is the eternal Witness which, though producing the appearance of everything, is not Itself a "thing." In that pure Awareness, the entire universe is perceived as a filmy illusion formed of 'nothing,' yet He who perceives it IS; He is the one and only Reality in whom all the drama of duality takes place. He is the perceiver and the perceived, the knower and the known, the subject and the object, on every stage of worldly experience. Nothing exists but that one Existence, that one pure and undisturbed Awareness; it is He alone who performs all this drama of multiplicity in Himself.

CHAPTER FOUR

Knowledge And Ignorance

1. By destroying ignorance,
   Knowledge reigns supreme --
   Like the wakefulness that destroys sleep.

2. By looking in a miror, one perceives his own identity;
   But that identity was already there.

3. In the same way, (relative) knowledge gives the understanding
   Of the identity of the world and the Self --
   But it is like using a knife
   To cut another knife.

4. If a person enters a house,
   And then sets it on fire,
   He gets burned along with the house.
   If a thief gets into a sack
   And then fastens it shut,
   He is bound along with the sack.

5. Fire, in the process of annihilating camphor,
Annihilates itself as well;
This is exactly what happens to knowledge
In the process of destroying ignorance.

6. When the support of ignorance is taken away,
Knowledge spreads
To the extent that it destroys itself.

7. As the wick of an oil-lamp burns to its end,
The flame flares up more brightly then before.
But this brightness
Is nothing but its extinction.

8. Is the breast of a woman
At its peak of development or beginning to sag?
Is the jasmine bud in full bloom or beginning
to fade?
Who can say?

9. The cresting of a wave is but its fall;
The flash of a bolt of lightning
Is but its fading.

10. Likewise, knowledge,
Drinking up the water of ignorance,
Grows so large
That it completely annihilates itself.

11. If the final deluge were to occur,
It would engulf all water and all space,
And leave nothing outside of it.

12. If the disc of the Sun
Were to become larger than the universe,
Both darkness and light would merge
In that all-pervading light.

13. Awakening dispels sleep,
And then it dispels itself,
Becoming the steady state of wakefulness.

14. In the same way,
That knowledge which shines
By virtue of the existence of ignorance
Is swallowed up by absolute Knowledge.

15. This absolute Knowledge is like
The intrinsic fullness of the moon,
Which is unaffected
By its apparent waxing and waning.

16. Or one might compare It to the Sun,
Which is never illuminated by any other light
Nor ever cast into darkness.

17. For that absolute Knowledge also
Is not revealed by another kind of knowledge
Or darkened by ignorance.

18. But can that pure Consciousness be conscious of Itself?
Can the eye look at itself?

19. Can space pervade space?
Can fire burn fire?
Can a man climb onto his own head?

20. Can vision perceive itself?
Does taste taste itself?
Can sound listen to itself?

21. Can the Sun shine on itself?
Can a fruit enjoy its own sweetness?
Can fragrance smell itself?

22. Likewise, that which is Consciousness Itself
Does not possess the quality of being conscious,
And is, therefore, not conscious of Itself.

23. If absolute Knowledge required the aid
Of some other kind of knowledge [to know Itself],
It would be nothing but ignorance.

24. Of course, light is not darkness;
But, to itself, is it even light?

25. Likewise,
He is neither existence nor non-existence.
By saying this,
It may seem that I'm saying, "He is not;"

26. But if it were true
That nothing at all exists,
Then who would know that there is nothing?

27. By what means might one prove
The theory of Nihilism?
It is a totally unjustified imputation
To the ultimate Reality.

28. If the extinguisher of a light
Were extinguished along with the light,
Who would know that there was no light?

29. If a person ceased to be
During the period of sleep,
Who would know that it was a sound sleep?

30. If there is a pot, a pot is perceived,
And if the pot is broken, its brokenness is perceived;
If there is no pot at all,
Is not its absence perceived as well?

31. It can be seen, therefore,
That he who perceives that there is nothing
Does not himself become nothing.
The Self has this same unique kind of existence,
Beyond both existence and non-existence.

32. The ultimate Reality
Is neither an object to Itself
Nor is It an object to anyone else.
Should It then be regarded as non-existent?

33. If a person falls asleep in a remote forest,
He is unperceived by anyone else.
Since he is asleep,
He, too, is unaware of his existence.

34. Nevertheless, he does not become lifeless,
Without existence.
Pure Existence is like this also;
It does not fit into the concepts
Of 'existing' or 'not-existing.'

35. When one's vision is turned inward,
One no longer perceives external objects,
But one does not therefore cease to exist
And to know he exists.

36. A very dark-skinned person
May stand in pitch-black darkness;
Neither he nor anyone else may be able to
perceive him.
Still, he certainly exists
And is aware of his existence.

37. However,
The existence of the Self
Is not like the existence or non-existence
Of a person;
He exists in Himself in His own way.

38. When the sky is clear of clouds,
It is without form;
But still the sky is there.

39. In a tank, the water may be so clear
That it appears non-existent;
Though one who looks into the tank may not
see it,
Still it is there.

40. Similarly,
The ultimate Reality exists in Itself,
And is beyond the conceptions
Of existence or non-existence.

41. It is like the awakeness that exists
When there is neither a remembrance
Of the sleep that has vanished
Nor the awareness of its own existence.

42. When a jar is placed on the ground,
We have the ground with a jar;
When the jar is taken away,
We have the ground without a jar;

43. But, when neither of these conditions exists,
The ground exists in its unqualified state.
It is in this same way
That the ultimate Reality exists.

Chapter Five: Introductory Note

In Chapter Five, Jnaneshvar begins with a clarification of the age-old designation of Brahman (the Absolute) as Satchidananda, *a composite Sanskrit word made up of* Sat *("Existence" or "Being"),* Chit *("Consciousness") and* Ananda *("Bliss"). It is a useful designation, as Jnaneshvar points out, because it includes in one word three separate aspects, or attributes, of the One. If we say merely that It is Existence, we leave out mention of the fact that It is Consciousness; if we refer to It merely as Consciousness, we leave out mention of the fact that It is pure satisfaction, or Bliss; and so on. But his purpose here is to explain that these three designations are merely hints, and are really inadequate, as all words are, to accurately describe the experience of the Absolute, of Brahman. "Whatever may be said about Him," says Jnaneshvar, "He is not that."*

Such words as "Consciousness," "Existence," "Bliss," suggest to us those states which are the opposite of "unconsciousness," "non-existence," and "unhappiness." This is the limitation of all language; it is based upon the dualism of contraries which we experience in the world. But the Absolute is beyond all contraries, and cannot be expressed in language. We can only say, "not this, not that."

Finally, in the last few verses, Jnaneshvar acknowledges that all his wordy outpourings are of no use in affecting anything at all; even such terms as "bondage" and "liberation" have no meaning in regard to the Self, the Absolute, Who remains always in the same state of Freedom. Nothing, therefore, is to be accomplished by all his lengthy explanations. The fact is, it is all for his own pleasure and delight in expounding the Truth.

CHAPTER FIVE

Existence, Consciousness, Bliss

1. These three attributes, *Sat, Chit,* and *Ananda*
(Existence, Consciousness, and Bliss),
Do not actually define Brahman.
A poison is poison to others,
But not to itself.

2. Shininess, hardness, and yellowness,
Together signify gold.
Stickiness, sweetness, and viscosity,
Together signify honey.

3. Whiteness, fragrance, and softness,
Are not three separate things,
But only camphor.

4. Camphor is white;
Not only that, it is soft.
And not only that, it is fragrant as well.

5. Just as these three qualities signify
One object -- camphor, and not three objects;
So the three qualities,
Sat, Chit, and Ananda,
Are contained in one reality.

6. It is true that the words,
"Sat," "Chit," and "Ananda,"
Are different,
But the three are united in one Bliss.

7. Sat is Ananda and Chit --
Or is it that Chit is Sat and Ananda?
They cannot be separated;
Just as sweetness cannot be separated from honey

8. The moon in the sky appears to pass through
Increasing stages of fullness,
But the moon is always the same;
It is always full.

9. When water is falling in drops,
We can count them.
But when the water is gathered
In a puddle on the ground,
It is impossible to count the number of drops.

10. In the same way,
The scriptures describe Reality
As *Sat,* or Existence,
In order to negate Its non-existence.
They call It *Chit,* or Consciousness,
In order to negate its unconsciousness.

11. The Vedas,
Which are the very breath of the Lord,
Declare It to be *Ananda,* or Bliss,
Only in order to negate the possibility
Of pain existing in It.

12. "Non-existence" is merely the counterpart,
Or opposite, of "existence."
The latter word is used
Only to differentiate it from the former.

13. Thus, the word, "Satchidananda,"
Used to refer to the Self,
Does not really describe Its nature,
But merely signifies
That It is not the opposite of this.

14. Can those objects which are illumined
By the Sun
Illumine the Sun himself?

15. How, then, could speech elucidate That
By the light of which
Speech itself is illumined?

16. What means of knowledge would be useful
To the self-illuminating Self,
Who is not an object of anyone's knowledge
And Who has no ability to know?

17. The means of knowledge is limited
By the object of knowledge.
It has no use in the case of That
Which is the subject.

18. The fact is, if we try to know *That,*
The knowledge itself is *That.*
How, then, could the knowledge
And the object of knowledge remain separate?

19. So, the words, "Sat," "Chit," and "Ananda,"
Do not denote *That;*
They are merely inventions of our thought.

20. These well-known words, "Chit," "Sat," and "Ananda,"
Are popularly used, it is true;
But when the knower becomes
One with That to which they refer,

21. Then they vanish
Like the clouds that pour down as rain,
Or like the rivers which flow into the sea,
Or like a journey when one's destination is reached.

22. A flower fades
After it gives birth to the fruit;
The fruit is gone
After it gives up its juice;
And the juice is gone
After it gives satisfaction.

23. A hand is drawn back
After the offering of oblations;
A melody ends after giving enjoyment.

24. A mirror is put aside
After showing to a face its reflection;
And a person goes away
After having awakened one who is asleep.

25. Similarly, these three,
Chit, Sat, and Ananda,
After awaking the seer to his Self,
Disappear into silence.

26. Whatever may be said about Him --
He is not that.
It is not possible to speak about His real nature,
Just as it is impossible
For one to measure himself
By taking the measurement of his shadow.

27. For when the measurer
Becomes conscious of himself,
He feels ashamed,
And gives up trying to measure himself
By his shadow.

28. Of course, what exists cannot be said not to exist;
But can such existence be called "Existence?"

29. Can what has become conscious
By destroying unconsciousness
Truly be called "Consciousness?"

30. In perfect wakefulness
There is neither sleeping nor waking;
Likewise, there is no consciousness
In the pure, absolute, Consciousness.

31. In blissfulness
There is no feeling of unhappiness;
But can it, for that reason, be called "Bliss?"

32. Existence vanishes along with non-existence,
Consciousness along with unconsciousness,
And bliss along with misery;
In the end, nothing remains.

33. Discarding the veil of duality
And all the pairs of opposites,
That alone remains
In Its own blessed state.

34. If we count It as one,
It appears to be something other
Than the one who counts.
Not from the viewpoint of enumeration,
But from the absolute viewpoint,
It is One.

35. If It were able
To be something other than Bliss,
It could enjoy bliss.
But since It is Itself Bliss,
How can it enjoy?

36. When the drum of worship is beaten,
The worshipper hears it as sound.
But when there is no worshipper,
That sound of beating
Does not hear itself.

37. Likewise, He, being Bliss Himself,
Cannot experience His bliss.
And, for the same reason,
He is not aware that He cannot.

38. If a face does not look into a mirror,
There is neither a face before it
Nor behind it.
Likewise, He is neither happiness nor misery,
But pure Bliss itself.

39. Abandoning all so-called illuminating concepts
As but jabberings in a dream,
He conceals Himself
From even His own understanding.

40. Even before the sugar cane is planted,
The juice is within it;
But its sweetness is unknown --
Except to itself.

41. Even before the strings of the Vina are plucked,
The sound is within it;
But that sound remains unknown,
Except to itself.

42. If a flower wished to enter into itself
In order to enjoy its own fragrance,
It would have to become a bee.

43. The flavor of food which is yet to be prepared
Is as yet unknown, except to itself.

44. So, can *That*, which does not even enjoy
Its own blissfulness,
Be tasted or enjoyed by others?

45. When the moon is overhead at noontime,
She cannot be perceived, except by herself.

46. It is like talking about beauty
Before it is given form,
Or youth before the birth of the body,
Or religious merit prior to any good actions;

47. Or sexual desire before it becomes
Manifest as tumescence;

48. Or the talk about the sound of a Vina
Which is not yet constructed,
And so is unknown, except to itself;

49. Or of fire
Which has not yet contacted fuel,
But only itself.

50. Only those who are able to see
Their own faces without a mirror
Are capable of understanding
The secret of the self-reflecting Reality.

51. Such talk as this
Is like discussing the harvest in storage
Before the seeds have been sown.

52. Pure Consciousness is beyond
Both generalizations and particular statements;
It remains ever-content in Itself.

53. After such a discourse,
That speech is wise
Which drinks deeply of silence.

54. It can be seen
That the various methods of proof
Have accepted their own unprovability,
And analogies have solemnly declared
Their inability to represent the Reality.

55. The various arguments have dissolved themselves
Because of their own invalidity,
And the assembly of definitions has dispersed.

56. All of the various means,
Having proved futile, have departed;
And the experience itself
Has abandoned its object.

57. Thought, along with its intent,
Has died,
Like a courageous warrior
In the cause of his master;

58. And understanding,
Ashamed of its own mode of knowing,
Has committed suicide.
The experience -- abandoned to itself alone --
Is like one beaten and crippled in battle.

59. When the crust
Of a piece of talc is peeled off,
The talc itself disappears.

60. If a plantain tree, troubled by the heat,
Casts off its outer layers,
How shall it stand erect?

61. Experience depends on the existence
Of the experienced and the experiencer.
When both of these vanish,
Can the experience alone experience itself?

62. Of what use are words
When even the experience
Dissolves itself in this way?

63. How can words describe the supreme Reality
Where even the subtlest speech itself disappears
And there is left no trace of sound?

64. Why should there be any talk
About waking a person who is already awake?
Does one begin to cook his food
After he has taken his meal and become satisfied?

65. When the Sun rises,
The light of the lamps is not needed.
Is there a need for a plough
At the time of harvest?

66. Truly, there is neither bondage nor freedom;
There is nothing to be accomplished.
There is only the pleasure of expounding.

Chapter Six: Introductory Note

In this chapter, Jnaneshvar praises the glory of the "word" as a means of recalling, through speech, the awareness of the Self. The word is the means whereby we transform the one Consciousness into thought, destroy our ignorance, and lead ourselves once again to the pure Consciousness of the Self. But, as Jnaneshvar points out, in that pure Awareness Itself, the word is superfluous, and moreover, futile. That pure Knowledge called the Self always IS, always remains. Therefore, he asks, where is this thing called "ignorance," which is to be banished by the word? It is but an imaginary superimposition upon the one Reality.

*Jnaneshvar then enters into an elaborate discussion of the paradoxical nature of ignorance (*ajnana*). While knowledge is obscured, ignorance has the semblance of existence; but when the true Knowledge is experienced, ignorance is nowhere to be found; it is seen to be a chimera with no real existence. It is but the contrary of knowledge. Elsewhere, in other contexts, Jnaneshvar does not hesitate to use the word, "ignorance," as though it were a definitive reality to be dispelled by knowledge; but here, his purpose is to reveal its essential illusoriness, i.e., its non-reality. His intention, of course, is to reveal That which does exist by negating what does not exist. In his own unmistakable style, he spouts analogy after homely analogy to bring home his point, leaving the mind boggled and reeling under the weight of the many word-pictures trooped out to support his relentless logic.*

The concept that ignorance is the impediment to Self-knowledge, and must be destroyed by knowledge, has a long history in the Vedantic tradition. It was often stated in the writings of the great 10th century Vedantist, Shankara, and had no doubt become, by Jnaneshvar's time, a hackneyed formula in the mouth of every jaybird philosopher. Great truths lose their significance and efficacy when they become mere formulized phrases to be repeated by schoolboys; and it was Jnaneshvar's purpose in taking up this subject to turn the old formulas inside out, and to stir the mind from its complacent rut, to a genuine self-inquiry.

THE WORKS OF JNANESHVAR

In every time, those who have experienced the Self are faced with the legacy of past expressions of this knowledge which have become calcified, as it were, into stone walls of tradition, standing in the way of real self-inquiry. The teachings of the Vedas, of the Buddha, and of Shankara, which burst those walls of complacent doctrine in their own time, themselves became in time bulwarks of meaningless doctrine which also had to be burst asunder by subsequent seers. In speaking of the Self, words, after all, are inadequate, and are therefore always open to contradiction. It is thus the perennial task of the enlightened to negate old terminologies, made meaningless by long familiarity, in order to jar awake the minds of men from their complacent slumber.

Jnaneshvar is just such an enlightened teacher. He appears to have demolished the old concepts of Shankara and the Vedantists, but the astute student will easily perceive that, when all the destruction is through and the dust has settled once more, Jnaneshvar has brought us to the same destination to which Shankara led us. After demolishing the old terms, "knowledge," and "ignorance," he points the way to the same inexpressible and supramental Knowledge to which Shankara pointed us. After denying the Vedantic concept of "superimposition," he leads us to the same two-in-One to which Shankara guided us. The terminologies of entrenched doctrine are continually being revealed as deceptive, and discarded by each new generation of seers -- like men attempting to peel the skins from a never-decreasing onion; yet the unnameable Truth which all are striving to reveal is one and the same, ever eluding their attempts to capture It in language.

Like all others before or after him who had succeeded in unwrapping the jewel of Self-knowledge, Jnaneshvar, in his attempt to reveal that jewel naked of wraps, succeeds only in presenting it wrapped in yet another fabric of mere words. Yet, his words, like those of other great teachers in possession of that jewel, possess an intrinsic transparency through which the lustre of Truth shines forth, exciting us with its beauty and inspiring in us the desire to make it our own.

CHAPTER SIX

Inefficacy Of The Word

1. When something is forgotten,
Either by ourselves or by another,
We are reminded of it by the word
Which we use to represent it.

2. If it had no other glory than this, however,
The word would not have so much value.

3. But the word,
Which, as everyone knows,
Serves as a reminder,
Is, in fact, a very useful thing.
Is it not a mirror which reflects
What has no form?

4. It is no great wonder that what is visible
May be seen in a mirror,
But in the mirror of the word,
What is invisible may be seen.

5. What the rising Sun is to the sky,
The word is to the sky of the Infinite.
That sky is illumined
By the power of the word.

6. The word is the flower
Of the sky of the Infinite;
Its fruit is the universe.
There is nothing
That cannot be determined by the word.

7. It is the torch-bearer that illumines
The path of right and wrong actions;
It is the judge that hands down
The decision between bondage or liberation.

8. When it sides with ignorance,
What is unreal appears real,
And the real becomes valueless.

9. The word causes the finite soul (*jiva*)
To enter into pure Consciousness (*Shiva*).

10. The word liberates the finite soul
Entangled in the body;
The Self meets Himself by means of the word.

11. The Sun, by giving birth to the day,
Becomes the enemy of night.
It cannot, therefore, be compared
To the word.

12. For the word supports at the same time
The path of action and the path of non-action --
Even though they are opposites.

13. It makes of itself a sacrifice
In order that the Self may be realized.
How can I describe
The many different merits of the word?

14. However, the word,
So well-known as a reminder,
Cannot coexist with the Self.

15. In the case of the Self,
Which is self-luminous and without support,
The word is absolutely useless.

16. There is nothing else beside the one Being.
Therefore, It cannot be the object
Of remembering or forgetting.

17. Can one remember or forget oneself?
Can the tongue taste itself?

18. To one who is awake, there is no sleep;
But is there awaking either?
In the same way,
There can be no remembering or forgetting
To the one Being.

19. The Sun does not know the night;
But can he know when it is day?
In the same way,
The one Being is without the ability
To remember or to forget.

20. Then what is the use of a reminder
Where there is no memory or forgetfulness?
You see, the word is of no use
In the case of the One.

21. However, there is a case where the word is
useful [as the destroyer of ignorance];
But I'm afraid even to think about this.

22. For it is foolish to say
That thc word destroys ignorance, [1]
And then the Self becomes conscious of Itself.

23. "The Sun will first destroy the night,
And then it will rise;"
Such a false notion could never be stated
Among intelligent people.

24. Where is that sleep
Which an already awakened person can banish?
Is there an awakening
For one who is already awake?

25. So, also, there is no ignorance to be destroyed.
There is no such thing as a Self
Desirous of becoming the Self.

26. Ignorance is as non-existent as the son
Of a barren woman.
Then what is there for "the sword
Of discrimination" to sever?

27. If the rainbow were as real as it seems,
What archer would not have strung it?

28. I could vanquish ignorance
By the power of logical thinking
If it were possible for the water of a mirage
To quench the thirst of Agastya. [2]

29. If ignorance was something
That could be destroyed by the word,
Then could we not set fire
To an imaginary city-in-the-sky?

30. Darkness cannot bear
Contact with a lighted lamp;
But was there really anything to be destroyed
Before the lamp was lit?

31. Also, it is futile to light a lamp
To illumine the light of day.

32. A shadow does not exist where it does not fall;
But it also does not exist where it does fall.

33. In the waking state,
One knows that the dream one saw was false.
Ignorance, also, though it appears to exist,
Does not exist.

34. What could one gain
By hoarding the wealth conjured by a magician?
Or by stealing the clothes
Of a naked beggar?

35. It is nothing more than fasting,
Even though one might eat an imaginary
sweet
A hundred-thousand times.

36. There is no moisture in the soil
Where there is no mirage;
But is there moisture where there is one?

37. If ignorance were as real as it seems,
Men would have been drenched
By the rain painted in a picture;
Fields would have been irrigated with it,
And reservoirs would have been filled.

38. Why should anyone bother to manufacture ink
If it were possible to write
With a preparation made from darkness?

39. Does not the sky appear blue to the eyes?
The appearance of ignorance
Is just as false.

40. Ignorance declares by its very name (*ajnana*)
That it does not exist.

41. The fact that it cannot be defined
Suggests its imaginary nature.
Thus, ignorance itself proves its own non-existence.

42. If it really exists,
Why can it not be determined by thought?
If there is really a jar on the ground,
It leaves some mark on the earth.

43. It is not correct
To say that the Self is revealed
After the destruction of ignorance.
It is like saying that the Sun is revealed
After it destroys its awareness of darkness.

44. Ignorance, though illusory,
Conceals its illusory nature;
And then it proves its own absence.

45. Thus, as has been shown in various ways,
Ignorance is, by its very nature, non-existent.
Then whom should the word destroy?

46. If one strikes one's shadow,
One strikes only the ground.
Nothing is damaged by slapping empty space --
Except one's own arm.

47. One may eagerly seek
To drink the water of a mirage,
Or to embrace the sky,
Or to kiss one's own reflection;
But all these efforts will be in vain.

48. The logic that tries to destroy ignorance
Is in the same category.

49. If there is one who still has a desire
To destroy this ignorance,
He may, at his leisure,
Peel the skin off the sky,

50. Or get milk from the [false] nipple of a billy-goat,
Or see with his knees,
Or dry out the night to make a blackboard;

51. Or he may squeeze the juice out of a yawn,
And, mixing it with laziness,
Pour it in the mouth
Of a man without a head.

52. He may reverse the flow of a stream,
Turn over his shadow,
Or make a rope of the wind.

53. He may thrash an imaginary ogre,
Tie up his reflection in a bag,
Or merrily comb the hair on his palm.

54. He may destroy
A water-jar that doesn't exist,
Pluck the flowers that grow in the sky,
Or handily break the horns of a rabbit.

55. He may prepare ink from camphor,
Gather soot from the lamp-flame of a jewel,
Or happily get married to
The daughter of a childless woman.

56. He may feed Chakor birds
With the nectar-rays of the New-moon,
Or easily catch the waterfowl
On the lake of a desert mirage.

57. What more need I say?
Ignorance is made of non-existence.
Then what is there for the word to destroy?

58. The word cannot prove its own existence
By destroying what does not exist;
Darkness cannot be made to comprehend
The nature of darkness.

59. Ignorance was never born.
So what is the point of discussing its
destruction?
It is like lighting a lamp
In the courtyard at noon.

60. They who think to gather the harvest
Before they have sown the seed
Gather only shame.

61. One may as well
Sit at home and do nothing
As beg from a naked beggar.

62. The illumination provided by the word
Does nothing to destroy ignorance;
It is like rain pouring on the ocean.

63. One may call oneself a measurer
So long as one does not try to measure the sky.
If light enables one to perceive darkness,
It is of no use.

64. If a tongue were able to taste
A dish made from the sky,
It would be meaningless
To call it a tongue.

65. Will the gaily-colored garments
Of a married woman
Be of any use at her husband's funeral?
To eat the core of the plantain tree
Is to eat nothing.

66. What object is there,
Small or large,
Which is not illumined by the Sun?
But even he is of no use at night.

67. What is there that is not
Perceived by the eyes?
But even they cannot perceive
The sleep in a person who is awake.

68. Though the Chakora bird
May look for the moon all day,
Its efforts are in vain.

69. One who reads from a blank sheet of paper
Is the same as dumb;
One who walks in the air
Is the same as lame.

70. In the same way,
Words, attempting to destroy ignorance,
Are but a meaningless jabbering.

71. On the night of the New-moon,
The moon sheds only darkness.
Thought, attempting to destroy ignorance,
Is in the same condition.

72. To make a meal of that food
Which is not yet prepared
Is the same as fasting.
To see with eyes that have lost their sight
Is the same as blindness.

73. That word which attempts to explain
The meaning of something that doesn't exist
Only accomplishes its own destruction.

74. Now, should I even say
That ignorance doesn't exist?
The word that negates it
Negates itself.

75. If thought stands in front of ignorance,
It destroys itself along with ignorance.

76. Ignorance, by its non-existence,
Prevents the word from being
Its vanquisher.

77. That the word should be so great
As to become the revealer of the Self
Is truly absurd.

78. Is there a place
Where one can marry himself?
Has there ever been a time
When the Sun eclipsed itself?

79. Can the sky be its own horizon?
Can the ocean enter itself?
Can a palm touch itself?

80. Does the Sun illumine himself?
Does a fruit bear fruit?
Does a fragrance smell itself?

81. We can readily believe that all creatures drink water,
But can we believe that water drinks water?

82. Has there ever been a day,
In all the three-hundred and sixty five, of the ye
Which has been perceived by the Sun?

83. If Shiva is angry,
He may burn the three worlds,
But will he burn fire also?

84. Is it possible even for the Creator
To stand before Himself without a mirror?

85. It is certain that eyesight
Cannot perceive itself,
That taste cannot taste itself,
That a person who is awake
Cannot be awakened.

86. How can sandal paste wear itself?
Or a color decorate itself with color?
Or a pearl adorn itself with pearls?

87. Can a touchstone turn itself into gold?
Can a lamp give light to itself?
Can a flavor enjoy its own sweetness?

88. Shiva holds the moon on his head;
But can the moon wear the moon
On its own head?

89. Likewise, the glorious Self
Is, Itself, pure and perfect Knowledge;
And how can Knowledge know itself?

90. Being Knowledge itself,
He does not know how to know Himself.
It is as hard as it would be
For the eye to perceive itself.

91. Knowledge could know itself
If a mirror could reflect itself
To itself.

92. A knife may be able to pierce
Anything in the four quarters;
But can that knife pierce itself?

93. The tip of the tongue is very good
For tasting different herbs and seasonings;
But can it taste itself?

94. Does it therefore cease to be an organ of taste?
No. It is because it tastes
That it is an organ of taste.

95. So also, the Self,
Who is Knowledge, Existence, and Bliss,
Is self-evident.
How then can the word
Offer Him what is already His own?

96. The ultimate Reality
Does not prove or disprove Itself
With the help of some other kind of knowledge;
It is self-evident, being the knower,
And is beyond proof and disproof.

97. It is therefore groundless to believe
That the word is so great
As to enable the Self
To experience Himself.

98. A lamp that is lighted at midday
Neither dispels darkness nor sheds any light.
It is the same with the word.

99. Since ignorance is non-existent,
There can be no question of destroying it.
And since the Self is self-evident,
What is there to be proved at all?

100. Thus, being in both these ways useless,
The word disappears --
Like a stream in the waters
Of the universal Deluge.

101. Right understanding shows that the word
Cannot in any way approach the Self.

102. Just as it is meaningless to say
That a dragon is coming,
Or that the sky is clinging to your palm,

103. So also, the word, with all its associates,
Becomes a meaningless babbling --
Like a picture with all the colors painted wrong.

104. It should now be clear that knowledge and ignorance,
Whose very existence is dependent upon the word,
Are as real as the forests painted in a picture.

105. Just as a cloudy day vanishes
When the clouds disappear,
So do both knowledge and ignorance vanish
When the word disappears in the universal Deluge [of Consciousness].

Chapter Seven: Introductory Note

Now, as though he had never touched on the subject before, Jnaneshvar once more takes up the matter of the illusory nature of ignorance. In this, the longest chapter of Amritanubhav, *he belabors the issue of the non-existence of ignorance to a point which the reader may find excessive, but he does it with such obvious relish and enjoyment that one cannot help being drawn along with him in his orgy of metaphor and simile.*

It is the traditional Vedantic concept of a beginningless ignorance, co-existent and co-eternal with the absolute Self, that Jnaneshvar so strongly objects to. In the world-conception attributed to Shankaracharya and other representitives of the non-dualistic philosophy of Vedanta, the perception of the phenomenal world is attributed to ignorance; and, it is asserted, once this ignorance is removed, there is seen to exist nothing but the unembodied Absolute, the one undifferentiated, pure Consciousness.

In the literature of Vedanta, the analogy of a rope on the ground appearing to be a snake is often cited: the snake-appearance is unreal; it is caused by ignorance. But once this ignorance is dispelled, the reality is seen, and it is perceived that there never was a snake, but only the rope all along. In the same way, it is held, once the unitive Reality is experienced, the phenomenal universe is seen to have been a mere mirage, or illusion.

Well, Jnandev takes issue with this line of thinking, and states emphatically that there is no such thing as ignorance; that even this multitude of sense objects is only that Being, the one Self. For Jnaneshvar, there is One and One only. He objects to the notion that the perception of the multiple universe is caused by a second additional factor, whether it be called "ignorance," "Maya," "delusion," or "superimposition" -- all terms traditionally used to account for the world-appearance. He regards such terms as misleading, for, as he states, "The Cause and the effect are one."

For Jnaneshvar, the multitude of sense objects, far from being a superimposed illusion, is only that one Being, the Self; and the perception of objects, far from being caused by ignorance, is caused simply by the Lord's delight in perceiving Himself through Himself in the form of creatures. "It is not ignorance that causes the separation between the perceiver and the perceived," says Jnaneshvar; "truly, He is everything, and He is the Cause of everything." In Jnaneshvar's philosophy, there is no place for Maya, or illusion, for he wishes to dissolve the mental barriers which separate the world and God. His vision refuses to allow any disruption to the Unity that he sees spreading everywhere, whether with his eyes closed in meditation, or wakeful and active in the manifested world.

CHAPTER SEVEN

Refutation Of The Doctrine Of Ignorance

1. But for knowledge,
Ignorance would never have shown itself.

2. A firefly appears as a light
Only when it is in darkness.
The idea of a beginningless ignorance
Is utterly false.

3. Ignorance is no more independent [of its opposite]
Than is a dream or darkness.

4. Horses made of clay cannot be harnessed;
The jewelry conjured by a magician
Cannot be worn.

5. This ignorance,
Dragged from the house of knowledge,
Can do nothing.
Does a mirage appear in the moonlight?

6. What is called knowledge
Is nothing but [the corollary of] ignorance;
Each appears at the concealment of the other.

7. Enough of this preamble;
Let us begin our search for ignorance.
Then, by understanding the true nature
Of ignorance,
We will understand the falsity of knowledge.

8. If there is really ignorance
Within [absolute] Knowledge
Why does it not change Knowledge
Into ignorance?

9. For it is the inherent nature of ignorance
To delude the one in whom it dwells.

10. If it is claimed by some
That the sacred texts declare
That the Self contains ignorance
And is concealed by it,

11. I would answer:
If the seed of ignorance dwells
In that state where there is no rise of duality,
Who, then, knows that it exists?

12. Ignorance, being nescient,
Cannot know itself.
Can it be a witness to its own existence?

13. No one could state that ignorance
Is the cause of the knowledge of ignorance
Without becoming aware of the contradiction,
And thus being compelled to silence.

14. If ignorance deludes the knower, the Self,
Who, then, is there to regard it as ignorance?

15. And if it does not delude the knower,
Would it not be shameful to call it ignorance?

16. If the clouds really eclipsed the Sun,
Who would illumine them?
If a person were really annihilated by sleep,
Who would experience it?

17. If the one in whom ignorance resides
Becomes ignorant,
That ignorance would be indiscernible;

18. For that by which ignorance is discerned
Can never be ignorance itself.

19. It would make no sense to say
That there is a cataract in the eye,
But the eyesight is unimpaired.

20. If fuel does not burn
When it is enveloped by a wild fire,
It is useless as a fuel.

21. If there is darkness in a house
But the house is not darkened,
Then it cannot be called darkness.

22. Who would call that "sleep"
Which does not disturb the waking state?
Can that be called "night"
Which does not cause the daylight
To vanish?

23. The word, "ignorance," is meaningless
If the Self is pervaded by it,
And yet remains as It is.

24. Moreover, it would be logically incorrect
To say that ignorance
Resides in the Self.

25. Ignorance is the gathering of darkness,
And the Self is the mine of effulgence;
How, then, could they be mixed?

26. If waking and dreaming,
Remembering and forgetting,
Could go hand in hand;

27. If cold and heat
Could sleep together in the same bed,
Or if the Sun's rays could be tied
in a bundle
By a rope of darkness;

28. Or if night and day
Came to live together in one place,
Then the Self might take ignorance
As its helpmate.

29. If death and life could reside together
As family-members,
Then the Self might become a dependent
Of ignorance.

30. How can it be said
That the very ignorance
That is dispelled by the Self
Lives happily with It?

31. However, if the darkness gives up its darkness,
And turns into light,
Then, of course, it becomes light.

32. Or if fuel gives up its state,
And turns into fire,
Then, of course, it becomes the fire.

33. Or if a small stream
Gives up its separate existence
By flowing into the Ganges,
Then it becomes the Ganges.

34. Thus, it is clear
That there is no ignorance;
There is only the Self.
For, as soon as ignorance
Comes into contact with Knowledge,
It becomes Knowledge.

35. Since ignorance is contrary to Knowledge,
It cannot retain its existence
Within Knowledge;
Nor can it exist independently.

36. If a fish made of salt
Were to become alive,
It could neither live in the water
Nor outside the water.

37. Therefore, such statements as,
"The Self shines when ignorance is vanquished,"
Should not be heeded by the wise.

38. The snake that is imagined
When one sees a rope,
Cannot be bound by the rope;
Neither can it be driven away.

39. Darkness, being frightened
By the approaching daylight,
Might turn for help to the full moon,
But it would be immediately
Swallowed up by that moon.

40. In the same way,
The word, "ignorance," is twice meaningless.
The nature of ignorance cannot be determined
Except by logical inference.

41. What, then, is its nature?
Is it only to be inferred
From the perceivable effects,
Or can it be directly apprehended?
Let us investigate.

42. Whatever may be apprehended
By the various modes of proof,
Like perception, and so forth,
Is the effect of ignorance
And not ignorance itself.

43. The creeping-vine has a beautiful sprout
Which goes straight up;
It is not a seed,
But the effect of the seed.

44. One may see both pleasant
And unpleasant forms in a dream;
These are not sleep itself,
But the effects of sleep.

45. Though the moon is one,
It may be seen in the sky as two;
This is not defective eyesight,
But the effect of defective eyesight.

46. In the same way,
The subject, the object,
And the various means of proof,
Are the effects of ignorance,
And not the ignorance itself.

47. Therefore,
The various modes of proof,
Such as perception, and so forth,
Being themselves the effects of ignorance,
Certainly cannot apprehend ignorance.

48. If we regard the effects of ignorance
As ignorance itself,
Then even the senses of perception
Must be included as ignorance.

49. If that which appears in a dream
Is illusory,
Then is the perceiver of the dream
Also illusory?

50. If the effect of ignorance is also ignorance,
It is like sugar tasting its own sweetness,
Or collyrium putting on collyrium,
Or like a stake being impaled on itself.

51. Also,
If the effects are identical with the cause,
Then all is ignorance,
And who would know anything?

52. In such a state,
One could not imagine a knower
Or the known.
It would be like taking as evidence
The fish swimming in a mirage lake.

53. So, my dear friend,
What cannot be measured or defined
By any proof whatsoever
Is not different from a sky-flower.

54. Ignorance
Does not allow of any proof of its existence.
So how could one begin to discuss it?
From this, one should understand
The impossibility of ignorance.

55. Ignorance,
Being neither an object of perception,
Nor of inference,
Is therefore disproved.

56. I am afraid to believe in this ignorance,
Since it is neither the cause of anything,
Nor the producer of any effect.

57. It can neither cause the Self to dream,
Nor can it put Him to sleep
In his place of repose.

58. Nonetheless,
Some say ignorance exists in the pure Self,

59. As fire exists in wood
Before two pieces of it are rubbed together.

60. But the pure Self
Does not even admit the name "Self!"
How could ignorance expect to find room there?

61. Can a flame be snuffed out
Before it is lit?
Or can we leave the shade of a tree
That has not yet sprouted?

62. Or smear salve on a body
That is not yet born?
Or cleanse a mirror that is not yet constructed?

63. Or skim the cream
From milk that's still in the udder?

64. So, likewise,
How can there be ignorance in the Self
Where there is not even room
For calling it "the Self"?

65. It should be clear
That ignorance does not exist.
And I wonder if it is even proper
To give it the semblance of existence
By stating that it does not exist.

66. If, in spite of this,
One continues to say
That ignorance exists in the Self,
Which is beyond all existence and non-existence,

67. It is like saying that an imaginary water-pot
Has broken into a hundred pieces,
Or that death itself had been utterly slain;

68. Or that unconsciousness had become unconscious,
Or that darkness had fallen into a dark well;

69. Or that non-existence was in a quandary,
Or that the core of a plantain tree was broken,
Or that the sky, by turning into a whip,
Was making a cracking sound;

70. Or that a dead man was being poisoned,
Or that one who could not speak
Was silenced,
Or that unwritten letters were erased.

71. It is false to say
That ignorance resides in the Self;
It is tantamount to saying
That they are identical.

72. But, can a barren woman have a child?
Can burnt seeds sprout?
Can darkness join the Sun?

73. No matter how we try
To find ignorance in the Self,
Which is pure Intelligence,
It cannot be found.

74. One may stir up the milk to find the cream,
But will it rise to the surface
Or will it disappear?
The search for ignorance is like this.

75. One may wake up quickly
In order to catch hold of sleep,
But will it be caught
Or will it be inadvertently destroyed?

76. Therefore,
Why should one madly search for ignorance?
Such searching is equal to not searching at all.

77. The village of understanding
Cannot be illumined in any way
By the existence of ignorance.

78. Have the eyes of understanding
Ever been able to see ignorance
Either within or outside of the Self?

79. The face of discrimination
Has never been washed by ignorance;
Nor has ignorance ever admitted of proof
Even in a dream.
In fact,
The thought that tries to grasp it,
Loses itself.

80. Do you, in spite of all this,
Think you will find some way to grasp ignorance?

81. You may as easily
Build a town hall out of rabbit horns,
And light it with the rays of the New moon;

82. And celebrate
By decorating the children of barren women
With sky-flowers.

83. The desire to discover ignorance
Will be fulfilled
When we're able to fill the cup of the sky
With the butter made from a turtle's milk.

84. We have tried in so many ways
To discover ignorance;
How many more times must we repeat
That it doesn't exist?

85. I would not utter the word, "ignorance,"
Even in a dream.
But I have a thought about it
Which I would like to share with you.

86. Suppose someone were to object in this fashion:
"You say that the ultimate Reality
Cannot see itself or any other object;

87. "Then how is it that It presents before Itself
The entire visible universe
And assumes the role of Witness to it?

88. "The entire universe arises
And is visible to us,
Who are, in fact, the Self.

89. "Though ignorance is not visible,
Still it exists without any doubt.
It is proved by inference
From the visible world!

90. "The moon is one;
If it appears in the sky as double,
Would we not infer
That our eyesight is impaired?

91. "The trees are fresh and green,
And yet, it would appear
That there is no water on the ground
From which they grow.

92. "Therefore, we infer
That their roots are absorbing water
From below.
Likewise, ignorance is inferred
By the appearance of the visible world.

93. "Sleep vanishes as soon as one awakes;
And though sleep is not known to the one who sleeps,
Still, its existence may be inferred
From the presence of dreams.

94. "So, if in the pure Self,
There appears this vast universe,
We naturally infer
The existence of ignorance."

95. To such an objection, I would reply:
How can this kind of knowledge
Be called "ignorance"?
Should we call daylight "darkness"?

96. Can that be called "collyrium"
Which, when smeared on an object,
Makes it as white and bright as the moon?

97. We may call this world
"The unfoldment of ignorance,"
If the full moon can be the cause
Of a dark night.

99. Can poison release nectarean love?
And if it does, can we call it "poison"?

100. Why should we bring in the tide of ignorance
When all that is unfolding before us
Is radiant with knowledge?

101. If we call this "ignorance,"
What shall we call "knowledge"?
Is the Self an object of either one?

102. The Self does not become anything.
He does not know what He is.
All the means of knowledge vanish in Him.

103. He is not such as can be said to exist,
Nor is there reason for saying He does not
exist.

104. He exists without the existence of 'another';
He sees without the existence of an object
Of vision.
This being so, why should we regard Him
As something to be found?

105. He silently endures
The conviction of the Nihilists
That He is nothing.
Nor is He disturbed by those who regard Him
As having particular attributes.

106. Do you think the omniscient One,
Who is the witness of even the deepest sleep,
Does not know about all of this?
Still, He does not become visible.

107. The Vedas have said the same,
Though they do not speak of the Self;
They say only "not this."

108. Whom does the Sun not illumine?
But does it illumine the Self?
Can the Self be contained beneath the sky?

109. The ego considers only the body,
Which is nothing but a bundle of bones,
And says, "This is who I am."
It takes no notice of the Self.

110. The intellect, which is able to grasp
Everything that can be known,
Falters before the Self.
The mind can imagine anything --
Except the Self.

111. The senses, that scrape their mouths
On the barren land of sense-objects,
Cannot taste the sweetness of the Self.

112. Is it possible
To completely comprehend the Self
Who has filled His belly
With all that exists
As well as all that does not exist?

113. Just as a tongue cannot taste itself,
So the Self
Cannot be an object of knowledge to Himself.
How, then, could He be an object to others?

114. As soon as ignorance,
With all her innumerable names and forms,
Approaches the Self,
It vanishes out of fear.

115. How can anything else
Find room in the Self?
He does not even desire to see
His own reflection.

116. There is a string-puzzle
Which appears to ensnare a stick;
But when the string is pulled,
The onlooker is amazed
To find that the stick is outside the puzzle.
The effort to determine the nature of the Self
Ends in the very same way.

117. One who minutely examines
His own shadow,
And then tries to jump over it,
Has failed to understand its nature.

118. Likewise, the person who,
After attempting to know the Self,
Comes to this or that conclusion,
Has failed to comprehend Its nature.

119. Words cannot even reach
To the place of the Self.
How, then, can the intellect
Comprehend Him as an object?

120. How can one acknowledge
The absence of sight in the Self,
And yet attribute vision to It?

121. He cannot experience His own existence
As an object of perception;
Therefore, He cannot be a perceiver.

122. In such a case,
Who will meet who?
How can there be vision
Where there is only One?

123. But He has flung open
The doors of perception in man,
And thus overcome this great obstacle!

124. Innumerable forms and visions arise,
But it is one pure Consciousness
Which is the substance of all.

125. The one, underlying, supreme Consciousness
Is so intoxicated by the great glory
Of this vision,
That He does not see Himself
In this mirror
Wearing the same jewelry twice.

126. He has so much of riches
That He causes Himself to appear
In a novel array each moment.

127. He regards the objects of the world,
Once created,
As old and uninteresting,
And therefore presents to His vision
Ever-new and freshly-created objects.

128. As the perceiving subject,
He is also incessantly changing
The ornaments of His perception.

129. For, being bored with the solitude
Of His original state,
He has become many.

130. Such is the all-knowing One.
As pure Consciousness,
He is full to the brim;
But that fullness is known
Only in His own house.

131. That pure Consciousness,
In whom knowledge and ignorance embrace,
Meets Himself by having vision
Of the many forms of the objective world.

132. Seeing the visible world,
He enjoys it as its witness.
That same bliss of enjoyment
Pervades the entire array.

133. The interplay of give and take goes on,
But the thread of unity is never broken.
The unity of a person's face
Is not altered by being reflected
In a mirror;

134. Nor is the standing position
Of a sleeping horse
Disturbed when it awakes.

135. Just as water plays with itself
By assuming the forms of waves,
The Self, the ultimate Reality,
Plays happily with Himself.

136. Fire weaves garlands of flames,
But is it thereby ensnared in duality?

137. Is the Sun separate from the rays
That radiate profusely from him?

138. Is the unity of the moon disturbed
By the glow of moonlight?

139. Though a lotus-blossom contains
A thousand petals,
Still it is one.

140. In mythology,
The king, Sahasrarjuna,
Had a thousand hands.
Did he then become
A thousand different beings?

141. On a loom, many strands may be interwoven;
But they are all only cotton.

142. Though a speech contains
Ten thousand words,
It is nothing but speech.

143. Though there are multitudes
Of visible objects,
And wave upon wave of images,
Still, they are not different
From their witness.

144. You may break a lump of raw sugar
Into a million pieces;
Still, there is nothing but sugar.

145. Likewise, the Self,
Though He perceives images,
Or manifests Himself
In the forms of manifold objects,
Does not become thereby a different thing.

146. The unity of the Self is not lost,
Even though He fills the whole universe.

147. Though a silk shirt
May be made of many colors,
With even a two-toned border,
It consists, after all, only of thread.

148. If the eye were able to see the whole universe
Without opening its lids,

149. Or if a banyan tree were able to reach maturity
Without sprouting from its seed,
This would be comparable to
The expansion of the One into many.

150. When He fervently desires to see Himself no more,
He reposes within Himself.

151. It is comparable to the absorbing
Of vision into itself
When the eyelids are closed;

152. Or to the fullness of the ocean
Even before the hightide;
Or to the withdrawing of
A tortoise's legs into itself;

153. Or to the withdrawal of the moon's light
On the night of the New moon.

154. It is not that the Self is "the destroyer,"
As He is falsely called,
When He withdraws both the witness
And the visible objects;
It is simply that He is reposing in Himself.

155. There is no doubt that the Self
Is all that exists.
Therefore, who is perceiving what?
The state of non-perceiving
We can call His sleep.

156. If He says to Himself,
"I don't care for this state of non-perception;
I want to see Myself!"
Then He becomes an object to Himself.

157. The Self is eternally the perceiver,
And eternally the perceived.
Now, what else needs to be created?

158. Does emptiness need to be attached to the sky?
Does the breeze need to be imparted to the air?
Does brightness need to be assigned to light?

159. The Self, shining as the universe,
Perceives the universe.
When there is no universe,
He perceives its non-existence.

160. And if, by chance,
The existence and non-existence
Of the universe
Were both to be perceived at once,
He alone is the perceiver
Of this state as well.

161. Does camphor derive its coolness
From the moonlight?
Is it not its own coolness?
Likewise, the Self is His own seer.

162. What more needs to be said?
Whatever condition the Self may be in,
He is seeing only His own Self --

163. Like one who discovers various countries
In his imagination,
And goes wandering through them all
With great enjoyment;

164. Or like a man who,
Pressing his closed eyelids with his fingers,
Perceives a pure brilliant light
Vibrating within.

165. When it is always only
The one pure Consciousness seeing Itself,
Why postulate the necessity
Of a superimposition? [1]

166. Does one cover a jewel with sparkle?
Does gold need to decorate itself
With shininess?

167. Does sandal wood need
The addition of scent?
Does nectar need flavor?
Does sugar need sweetness?

168. Does camphor need
To be smeared with whiteness?
Or does fire need to be heated
In order to make it hot?

169. A creeping vine,
Entwining about itself,
Forms its own bower.

170. A lamp that is lit
Does not need the addition of light;
It is resplendent with light.
Likewise, the one pure Consciousness
Is resplendent with radiance.

171. Therefore,
Without obligation to anything else,
He easily perceives Himself.

172. Perceiving and non-perceiving
Are the same to Him.
Is there any difference to the moon
Between darkness and light?

173. Whether he desires one or the other,
He is always of the same nature.

174. For a while, the Self appears
As an object of perception;
But when the seer and the seen unite,
Both of them vanish.

175. Then the seen is the same as the seer;
The seer is merged in the seen.
Both vanish,
And only the Reality remains.

176. At any place and at any time,
The seer and the seen
May embrace each other, and merge.

177. Camphor does not become fire,
Nor does fire become camphor;
Both of them
Are destroyed at the same time.

178. In mathematics,
When one is subtracted from one,
What's left is zero --
And then that is erased.
The same thing happens
When the seer and the seen unite.

179. If someone attempts to wrestle
With his own reflection in the water,
Both the wrestling and the reflection
Vanish together.

180. When the perceiver and the perceived
Meet and unite,
There is no more perception.

181. The eastern sea and the western sea
Are different
Only so long as they do not mingle.
But once they have intermingled,
There is only water.

182. Every moment, new triads
Of perceiver, perception and perceived,
Are emerging.
Does each one need to be analyzed?

183. Every moment,
A particular quality is swallowed up
And its opposite emerges.
This is the opening and closing
Of the eye of Reality.

184. How amazing it is
That when the eyelids are open,
The Self becomes a perceiver
Who vanishes when the eyelids are closed.

185. The natural state of the Self
Lies between the destruction
Of the perceiver and the perceived
And a new revival of them.

186. It is like the natural state of water
When the wave that has arisen subsides
And a new one has not yet arisen;

187. Or like the state
In which our sleep has ended,
But we are not yet fully awake;

188. Or it may be imagined
If we think of the sight
Which has ceased to look at one object
And has not yet begun to look at another.

189. It is like the state of the sky
When the day has ended,
But night has not yet come.

190. Or like the state of the *prana*
When one breath is finished
And a new one is not yet taken in;

191. Or the state of one whose senses
Are all enjoying their objects simultaneously.

192. This is what the ultimate nature of the Self
is like;
So, how can there be
Either seeing or non-seeing?

193. Can a mirror see its own polished surface?

194. By means of a mirror,
There is a face in front and a face behind;
But can that be so without a mirror?

195. The Sun sees everything;
But can he witness the beauty
Of his own rising and setting?

196. Can a juice drink itself?
Or does it hide from others in shame
On that account?
It can do neither of these things;
It is, itself, juice.

197. Likewise, He is vision itself;
He does not know seeing or non-seeing.
He, Himself, is the cause of both.

198. Being perception Himself,
How could He see Himself?
Of course, He is also non-perception.

199. How can non-perception perceive itself?
He is, Himself, non-perception.

200. These two: perception and non-perception,
Dwell happily together,
And each is the destroyer of the other.

201. If seeing were able to see itself,
Wouldn't this be like not-seeing?
He is not touched
By either seeing or not-seeing.

202. If the Self,
Who can neither be seen or not seen,
Sees --
Then, who has seen what?

203. If the visible world appears,
Then has it not been perceived by the seer?
No. For it is not due to the appearance
That He sees.

204. The appearance is seen, to be sure;
But the appearance is in fact
Nothing but the seer.
How can something else
That does not exist be seen?

205. Supposing someone sees his own face in a mirror;
That face actually exists in itself,
But what is seen is unreal.

206. It is like seeing oneself in a dream,
While asleep.

207. If someone dreams
That he is carried away in a vehicle
To some other place,
Is he really carried away?

208. Or if he dreams that a pair of headless beggars
Have taken over the kingdom,
Is it really so?

209. No. That person remains the same,
Despite the dream,
As he was prior to falling asleep.

210. The suffering of a thirsty person
Is the same after he finds a mirage
As it was before.
What has he gained?

211. Or if a person strikes up an aquaintance
With his own shadow --
Of what use is that?

212. The Self as a witness,
Has become the object of perception,
And then revealed it to Himself.
But the revealing is really irrelevant.

213. Because, if what is seen
Is nothing but the seer,
How can the seer benefit by that revelation?
Is He not present to Himself
Even when He is not revealed?

214. Does a face become something less
If it does not see itself in a mirror?
It is what it is,
Even without a mirror.

215. Likewise,
The Self is not diminished
If He is not revealed to Himself.
Such revelation is really of no consequence.

216. The Self is as He is,
Even without becoming a witness to Himself.
Now it may be protested:
"Why should He who is complete in Himself
Cause Himself to be an object of perception?

217. "It makes no sense to say
That what already exists is revealed;
Such revelation is pointless.

218. "It is the rope which actually exists,
Even though it appears as a snake.
It is the Witness who really exists,
Even though He appears
As the object of perception.

219. "When a mirror is held before one's face,
That face appears to be in the mirror;
But, in fact, the face is
In its own place and not in the mirror.

220. "Of these two: the seer and the seen,
It is the seer who really exists.
What is seen, though perceivable,
Has no reality."

221. And I would answer:
Indeed, it has no *independent* reality;
But it does appear.
Does this not seem to prove
That it has existence?

222. If a person sees some other object,
Then we have a seer, the seen,
And the act of seeing.

223. But in the case of the Self,
He sees nothing other than Himself --
Whether He looks or not,
Whether He remains one or many.

224. A face sees only itself,
Even though a mirror has revealed it.
And that face remains the same,
In itself,
Even when it is not revealed by a mirror.

225. It is the same with the Self:
When He is revealed, He is what He is;
When He is not revealed, He is the same.

226. Whether a person is awake or asleep,
He is the same person.

227. A king, reminded of his kingship,
Is certainly a king;

228. But is there any loss to his majesty
Even if he is not reminded?

229. In the same way,
The Self may be revealed or not revealed;
He does not become greater or lesser.
He always remains as He is.

230. Is there some other thing
Which is eagerly trying to reveal
The Self to Himself?
But for the Self,
Would there be a mirror?

231. Does a lit candle create
The person who lights it,
Or does it exist because of the person?
Truly, the Self is the Cause
Of all causes.

232. The flame lights the fire;
But can it be regarded
As something different from fire?

233. Whatever we call a "cause"
Is created and revealed by Him.
By His very nature,
He *is* whatever He sees.

234. The Self is self-illuminating.
Therefore, there is no other cause
For His seeing Himself
Than Himself.

235. Whatever form appears,
Appears because of Him.
There is nothing else here but the Self.

236. It is the gold itself which shines
In the form of a necklace or a coin;
They, themselves, are nothing but gold.

237. In the current of the river
Or the waves of the sea,
There is nothing but water.
Similarly, in the universe,
Nothing exists
Or is brought into existence
That is other than the Self.

238. Though it may be smelled,
Or touched, or seen,
There is nothing else in camphor
But camphor.

239. Likewise,
No matter how He experiences Himself,
The Self is all that is.

240. Whether appearing as the seen,
Or perceiving as the seer,
Nothing else exists besides the Self.

241. In the Ganges,
Whether it flows as a river
Or mingles with the ocean,
We cannot see anything added;
It is only water.

242. Whether it is liquid or frozen,
Ghee (clarified butter) does not become anything other than itself.
It would be foolish to think that it did.

243. Flames and fire
Are not seen as two separate things.
Flame is the same as fire
And is not different from it.

244. Therefore,
Whether He is the seer or the seen,
It doesn't matter;
There is only the Self
Vibrating everywhere.

245. From the standpoint of vibration,
There is nothing but vibration.
So, even though the Self sees,
Does he really see?

246. It is not that the appearance is arrayed
Here,
And the seer is over
There;
It is only His own vibration
That He perceives when He sees.

247. It is like ripples on water,
Or like gold on top of gold,
Or eyesight gazing at vision.

248. It is like adding music to music,
Or fragrance to fragrance,
Or bliss to bliss;

249. Or like pouring sugar on sugar,
Or covering a mountain of gold
With gold,
Or adding fire to the flames.

250. What more need I say?
It is like the sky reposing on the sky.
Who then is asleep?
And who is awake?

251. When He sees Himself,
It is as though He did not see.
And even without seeing Himself,
He goes on seeing Himself.

252. Here, speech is prohibited;
Knowledge is not allowed.
Pride of experience can gain no entry.

253. His seeing of Himself
Is like no one seeing nothing.

254. In short,
The Self is self-illuminating.
He awakens Himself without awaking.

255. Because of His desire to see Himself,
He manifests all the various states of being
Without affecting His own state.

256. If He wishes to remain without seeing,
Even that not-seeing
Is seeing.
And because of *that* seeing,
Both seeing and non-seeing disappear.

257. Though He may expand into any form,
His unity is never disturbed.
And if He contracts,
Then He is still as full as before.

258. The Sun can never catch up with darkness;
So, why should he listen
To talk about light?

259. Let there be darkness or light,
The Self is like the Sun
Who remains alone in his own glory
Under every condition.

260. The Self may assume any form;
He never strays from Himself.

261. Though innumerable waves rise
And fall on the ocean,
The ocean does not therefore become
Something other than the ocean.

262. We may not truly compare the Sun
To the glorious Self,
Who is pure Light,
Because the Sun's rays go out from himself.

263. Cotton cannot be compared to Him,
For there would be no cloth
If the cotton pods did not burst.

264. Unformed gold cannot be compared to Him,
For it cannot be made into ornaments
While remaining as it is.

265. No individual may be compared to Him,
For no one is able to go
From one country to another
Without crossing the intervening space.

266. So the play of the Self
Has no parallel.
He can be compared only to Himself.

267. He is incessantly devouring
Mouthfuls of His own light.
But neither is His store of light diminished,
Nor is His belly expanded.

268. The Self,
Through His incomparable sport,
Is ruling His own kingdom
Within Himself.

269. If this can be called "ignorance,"
It means the end of all logical thinking.
Can we be patient with someone who thinks
This way?

270. If That which illumines
Is called "ignorance,"
It is like calling a miner's lamp
"A black stone."

271. Would it make sense
To call a shining golden statue
Of the Goddess
"The Dark One"?
Giving the name, "ignorance,"
To the self-illumination of the Self
Is like this.

272. In truth, all beings and all elements,
From the gods to the smallest particle of earth,
Are illumined by His rays.

273. It is because of Him
That knowledge knows,
Sight sees,
And light illumines.

274. Who, then, is that mean person
Who has designated Him as "ignorance"?
Really!
Is it not like saying the Sun is tied up
In a sack of darkness?

275. To write the letter 'A'
Before the word, *jnana* (knowledge),
As a means of enhancing
The greatness of *jnana*!
Is that not an extraordinary method
Of expanding a word's meaning?

276. What's the point of placing a fire
In a cardboard box?
It will only turn that into flames
As well!

277. It is pointless to speak
About the notion of ignorance
When the whole universe
Is the vibration of Knowledge.

278. First, it's like believing there was a murder
Simply because someone cries out "murder!"
Secondly, such a notion is utterly false;
How can Knowledge be called "ignorance"?

279. Even to speak of ignorance
Is itself a vibration of Knowledge.
Then, mustn't we call this Knowledge
"Knowledge"?

280. By His own illumination,
The Self is perceiving Himself
In all these various forms.

281. How is it, then, that ignorance,
Which dissolves before the searchlight
Of thought,
Might acquire perception,
And see itself as the visible world?

282. If ignorance states
That it gives birth to the world,
Which is Knowledge,
And attempts to establish its existence
By means of ignorance,

283. Then the world itself
Has incontrovertibly proven
The non-existence of ignorance;
Because ignorance and Knowledge
Are not things which are related
In the way that a substance
And its quality are related.

284. Knowledge could be a quality of ignorance
If pearls could be made with water,
Or if a lamp could be kept lit with ashes.

285. Ignorance could emit the light of Knowledge
If the moon could emit leaping flames,
Or if the sky could be turned to stone.

286. It is certainly astounding
That a deadly poison
Could arise from an ocean of milk;
But, could a deadly poison
Give rise to pure nectar?

287. Even supposing
That ignorance were produced from Knowledge,
That ignorance would vanish at its very birth.
Then, again, nothing would remain but Knowledge.

288. Just as the Sun is nothing but the Sun,
The moon is nothing but the moon,
And the flame of a lamp
Is nothing but a flame --

289. Be assured also
That the light of Consciousness
Is nothing but Light.
The whole universe
Is nothing but the luminosity of the Self.

290. The scriptures declare with assurance
That everything that exists
Is radiating with His light.
Is it said for no reason?

291. The light of the Self
Is Itself the cause
Of the appearance of His beauty
Which He Himself is enjoying.

292. To ignore this truth,
And to regard ignorance as the cause
Of the Self's appearance to Himself
Is utterly unreasonable.

293. Ignorance cannot be found to exist
By any means.
No matter how we may search for it,
That search proves futile.

294. For, even if the Sun
Were to visit the house of night,
He would find no darkness;

295. Or, if a person attempted
To catch sleep in a bag,
He would find that
He could not even catch awakening;
He would remain just as he was.

Chapter Eight: Introductory Note

Having established the non-existence of ignorance in the absolute Consciousness, Jnaneshvar reiterates once more the obvious corrolary to this assertion: that knowledge, which is the complement to ignorance, does not exist in that state either. These two, knowledge and ignorance, exist only relative to each other; they are both illusory, and disappear in the unitive experience of the one Self.

CHAPTER EIGHT

The Refutation Of Knowledge

1. As for ourselves,
We possess neither knowledge nor ignorance.
Our Guru has awakened us
To our true Identity.

2. If we attempt to see our own state,
That seeing itself becomes ashamed.
What, then, should we do?

3. Fortunately,
Our Guru has made us so vast
That we cannot be contained
Within ourselves.

4. Our identity is not limited
Solely to the universal Self,
But we are not disturbed
By perceiving our separative existence;
We remain, after final liberation,
The same as we were before.

5. The word that can describe our state
Has not yet been uttered.
The eyes that can see us
Do not exist.

6. Who could perceive us,
Or enjoy us as an object of enjoyment?
We cannot even perceive ourselves!

7. The wonder is that we are
Neither concealed nor manifest.
Ah -- how amazing it is
That we even exist!

8. How can mere words
Describe the state
In which we are placed by Sri Nirvitti?

9. How can ignorance
Dare to come before us?
How can illusion
Come into being after its death?

10. And can there be any talk of knowledge
Where ignorance cannot gain entrance?

11. When night falls,
We light the lamps;
But what is the use of such efforts
When the Sun is here?

12. Likewise,
When there is no ignorance,
Knowledge also disappears;
Both of them have gone.

13. Actually,
Knowledge and ignorance are destroyed
In the process of discerning their meaning.

14. Both the husband
And the wife lose their lives
When each cuts off the other's head.

15. A lamp held behind a person
Is not really a light;
If it's possible to see in the dark,
It's not really darkness.

16. We may call that which is utter nescience
"Ignorance,"
But how can we call by the name of "ignorance"
That by means of which everything is known?

17. Knowledge turns into ignorance,
And ignorance is dispelled by knowledge;
Each is cancelled by the other.

18. Thus, he who knows does not know,
And even he who does not know, knows.
Where, then,
Could knowledge and ignorance dwell.

19. Since the Sun of Self-realization
Has arisen in the sky of pure Consciousness,
It has swallowed up
Both the day of knowledge
And the night of ignorance.

Chapter Nine: Introductory Note

In this Ninth chapter of Amritanubhav, *Jnaneshvar speaks of how all this world has arisen from the Lord's own expression of enjoyment. He has become all enjoyers and all objects of enjoyment; and one who realizes his identity as both enjoyer and enjoyed, both seer and seen, knows the joy of God. His enjoyment knows no bounds, for, even while enjoying sense-objects, he is aware that all objects of enjoyment are only Himself; he perceives, as Jnaneshvar does, that "unity is only strengthened by the expansion of diversity." This exalted awareness Jnaneshvar regards as the true freedom, or "liberation."*

For Jnandev, liberation is certainly not merely a dry, intellectual, unity-awareness; it is the enjoyment of the bliss, or love, of God. It is a Knowledge-Love; not a love based on the duality of lover and beloved, but rather an inner joyfulness that arises with the sense of union with the Beloved. Should there be, then, no devotion for the sage who is one with God? 'Why not?' asks Jnaneshvar; 'Does not a fruit tree enjoy its own blossoming? Does not love arise in the heart even when it is its own object?' There are no words for this "natural devotion" at which Jnandev hints. The lover and Beloved are one, to be sure; yet the enjoyment of love continues. This is Amritanubhav: *the nectar of the experience of our own divine Self.*

CHAPTER NINE

The Secret Of Natural Devotion

1. Just as a nose might become a fragrance,
Or ears might give out a melody
For their own enjoyment,
Or the eyes might produce a mirror
In order to see themselves;

2. Or just as cheeks might become a soft breeze,
Or a head might take the form
Of Champaka blossoms
In order to produce a sweet scent;

3. Or a tongue might become sweetness,
A lotus-bud might blossom as the Sun,
Or a Chakora bird might become the moon;

4. Or flowers might take the form of a bee,
A lovely young girl might become a young man,
Or a sleepy man might become
A bed on which to lie;

5. As the blossoms of a mango tree
Might become a cuckoo bird,
Or one's skin might become
Malayan breezes,
Or tongues might become flavors;

6. Or as a slab of gold might become
Articles of jewelry
For the sake of beauty,

7. Just so, the one pure Consciousness becomes
The enjoyer and the object of enjoyment,
The seer and the object of vision,
Without disturbing Its unity.

8. A Shevanti flower bursts forth
With a thousand petals,
Yet it does not become anything
But a Shevanti flower.

9. Similarly, the auspicious drums
Of ever-new experiences
May be sounding,
But in the kingdom of Stillness,
Nothing is heard.

10. All of the senses may rush simultaneously
Toward the multitude of sense objects,

11. But, just as, in a mirror,
One's vision only meets one's vision,
The rushing senses only meet themselves.

12. One may purchase a necklace,
Earrings, or a bracelet --
But it is only gold,
Whichever one receives.

13. One may gather a handful of ripples --
But it is only water in the hand.

14. To the hand, camphor is touch,
To the eye, it's a white object,
To the nose it is fragrance;
Nonetheless, it is camphor, and nothing but camphor.

15. Likewise, the sensible universe
Is only the vibration of the Self.

16. The various senses attempt to cath
Their objects in their hands --
For example, the ears
Try to catch the words;

17. But as soon as the senses
Touch their objects,
The objects disappear as objects.
There's no object for one to touch;
For all is the Self.

18. The juice of the sugarcane
Is part of the sugarcane;
The light of the full moon
Belongs to the full moon.

19. The meeting of the senses and their objects
Is like moonlight falling on the moon,
Or like water sprinkling on the sea.

20. One who has attained this wisdom
May say whatever he likes;
The silence of his contemplation
Remains undisturbed.

21. His state of actionlessness
Remains unaffected,
Even though he performs countless actions.

22. Stretching out the arms of desire,
One's eyesight embraces
The objects she sees;
But, in fact,
Nothing at all is gained.

23. It is like the Sun
Stretching out the thousand arms
Of his rays
In order to grasp darkness.
He remains only light, as before --

24. Just as a person, awakening to
Enjoy the activity of a dream,
Finds himself suddenly alone.

25. Even one who has attained wisdom
May appear to become the enjoyer
Of the sense-objects before him,
But we do not know
What his enjoyment is like.

26. If the moon gathers moonlight,
What is gathered by who?
It is only a fruitless
And meaningless dream.

27. That yoga which yogis attain
Through restraining the senses
And other ascetic practices,
When placed before this path,
Is like the moon
Placed before daylight.

28. There is really no action or inaction;
Everything that is happening
Is the sport of the Self.

29. The undivided One
Enters the courtyard of duality
Of His own accord.
Unity only becomes strengthened
By the expansion of diversity.

30. Sweeter even than the bliss of liberation
Is the enjoyment of sense objects
To one who has attained wisdom.
In the house of *bhakti* (devotion),
That lover and his God
Experience their sweet union.

31. Whether he walks in the streets
Or remains sitting quietly,
He is always in his own home.

32. He may perform actions,
But he has no goal to attain.
Do not imagine
That if he did nothing,
He would miss his goal.

33. He does not allow room
For either remembering or forgetting;
For this reason,
His behavior is not like that of others.

34. His rule of conduct is his own sweet will.
His meditation is whatever
He happens to be doing.
The glory of liberation
Serves as an *asana* (seat-cushion)
To one in such a state.

35. God Himself is the devotee;
The goal is the path.
The whole universe is one solitary Being.

36. It is He who becomes a god,
And He who becomes a devotee.
In Himself,
He enjoys the kingdom of Stillness.

37. The temple itself is merged
In the all-pervasive God;
The motion of time
And the vastness of space
Are no more.

38. Everything is contained
In the Being of God.
Where is there any room for the Goddess?
Neither are there any attendants.

39. If a desire
For the Master-disciple relationship arises,
It is God alone
Who must supply both out of Himself.

40. Even the devotional practices,
Such as *japa* (repetition of God's name),
Faith and meditation,
Are not different from God.

41. Therefore, God must worship God
With God,
In one way or another.

42. The temple, the idol, and the priests --
All are carved out of the same stone mountain.
Why, then, should there not be
Devotional worship?

43. A tree spreads its foliage,
And produces flowers and fruits,
Even though it has no objective
Outside of itself.

44. But what does it matter if a dumb person
Observes a vow of silence or not?
The wise
Remain steadfast in their own divinity
Whether they worship or not.

45. What's the point of worshipping with rice
An idol of the Goddess
That's made out of rice?

46. Will the flame of a lamp
Remain without light
If we do not ask her to wear
The garment of light?

47. Is not the moon bathed in light
Even though we do not ask her
To wear the moonlight?

48. Fire is naturally hot;
Why should we consider heating it?

49. A wise person is aware
That he, himself, is the Lord, Shiva;
Therefore, even when he is not worshipping,
He is worshipping.

50. Now the lamps of action and inaction
Have both been snuffed out,
And worshipping and not-worshipping
Are sitting in the same seat,
And eating from the same bowl.

51. In such a state,
The sacred scriptures are the same as censure,
And censure itself
Is the same as a sweet hymn of praise.

52. Both praise and censure
Are, in fact, reduced to silence;
Even though there is speech,
It is silence.

53. No matter where he goes,
That sage is making pilgrimage to Shiva.
And if he attains to Shiva,
That attainment is non-attainment.

54. How amazing!
That in such a state,
Moving about on foot
And remaining seated in one place
Are the same.

55. No matter what his eyes fall upon
At any time,
He always enjoys the vision of Shiva.

56. If Shiva Himself appears before him,
It is as if he has seen nothing;
For God and His devotee
Are on the same level.

57. Of its own nature,
A ball falls to the ground,
And bounces up again,
Enraptured in its own bliss.

58. If ever we could watch
The play of a ball,
We might be able to say something
About the behavior of the sage.

59. The spontaneous, natural devotion
Cannot be touched by the hand of action,
Nor can knowledge penetrate it.

60. It goes on without end,
In communion with itself.
What bliss can be compared to this?

61. This natural devotion is a wonderful secret.
It is the place in which meditation
And knowledge become merged.

62. Hari and Hara (Vishnu and Shiva)
Are, of course, really the same;
But now, even their names and forms
Have become identical.

63. Oh, and Shiva and Shakti,
Who were swallowing each other,
Are now both swallowed up
Simultaneously.

64. And even the subtlest speech,
Eating up all objects
And drinking up gross speech,
Has now taken its rest in sleep.

65. O blissful and almighty Lord!
You have made us the sole sovereign
In the kingdom of perfect Bliss.

66. How wonderful
That You have awakened the wakeful,
Laid to rest those who are sleeping,
And made us to realize
Our own Self!

67. We are Yours entirely.
Out of love,
You include us as Your own,
As is befitting Your greatness.

68. You do not receive anything from anyone,
Nor do You give anything of Yourself
To anyone else.
We do not know how You enjoy Your greatness.

69. As the Guru, you are the greatest of the great;
But You are also very light,
Capable of buoying up your disciples,
And thus saving them from drowning in the world.
Only by Your grace can these dual qualities
Of Yours be understood.

70. Would the scriptures have extolled You,
If, by sharing it with Your disciple,
Your unity were disturbed?

71. O noble One!
It is Your pleasure
To become our nearest and dearest
By taking away from us
Our sense of difference from You.

Chapter Ten: Introductory Note

Knowledge and ignorance, Shiva and Shakti, action and inaction, and all other such dualities, have been swallowed up in Unity. There, words fall short; names cannot name It. Where there is no two-ness, language is invalidated. Like others before him who have attempted to speak of It, Jnaneshvar finds himself in a cul-de-sac, forced to silence. Why, then, has he bothered to speak of It at all? He has no naive hopes or expectutions of being understood or of providing illumination to others. The Self reveals Itself, and cannot be revealed by any such words as these. But the very nature of the Self is Self-expression, and that expression can no more be repressed than can the Sun's radiating warmth, or the blossoming of the flowers in Spring.

Jnaneshvar's words are but the overflowing effulgence of the Self, and they contain the very sweetness of the Self. Fully aware of this, Jnaneshvar says, "Amritanubhav *is so pure and sweet that even the timeless state of Liberation yearns for a taste of it." This is The Nectar Of Mystical Experience which Jnaneshvar proffers for us to sip and enjoy. It is a gift for which we have reason to give thanks. To one who understands, its sweetness is beyond measure. It is, indeed, a gift of the divine Lord, offered so that we may savor and take delight in our own immeasurable Bliss.*

CHAPTER TEN

Blessings To The World

1. O Sri Nivrittinath!
You have blessed me
With such sublime Bliss!
Should I only enjoy it in myself?

2. The great Lord has endowed the Sun
With a fountain of light
With which he illumines the entire world.

3. Was the nectar of the moon's beams
Given only for the moon's sake?
Were the clouds given water by the sea
For their own use?

4. The lamp's light is meant
For the entire household;
The vastness of the sky
Is for the sake of the whole world.

5. Consider the surging tides
Of the unfathomable sea;
Are they not due to the power of the moon?
And it is the Spring season
Which enables the trees to offer
Their blossoms and their fruits.

6. Also, it is no secret
That all this is the gift
Of Your blissful divinity;
I have nothing of my own.

7. But why should I go on explaining like this?
I only get in the way
Of my Master's glory!

8. All that we have said
Is already self-evident.
Can words illumine the self-luminous?

9. Even if we had kept silence,
Would not some person have seen another?

10. When one person sees another,
It becomes self-evident
That the seer is also the seen.

11. There is no other secret
About pure Knowledge that this;
And this is self-evident
Before it is mentioned.

12. If it be said
that there was then no need
To begin to write such a work as this,
I would have to reply that
We are describing what is already self-evident
Only out of love for it.

13. It may be that we have tasted it before,
But there is a new delight
In tasting it again.
To speak of what is self-evident
Is therefore unobjectionable.

14. At least, I have not given out a secret;
It is self-revealed.

15. We are immersed in the one perfect 'I';
We are pervading everything.
Therefore, we can be neither concealed
Nor revealed by anything.

16. What can we offer ourselves
In the form of exposition?
Would the Self be unexposed
If we were to remain silent?

17. My speech is therefore the same
As the deadest silence.

18. Even the ten Upanishads
Cannot approach this silent speech;
There, the intellect becomes
Absorbed in itself.

19. Jnanadeva says,
"This is the sweet Nectar
Of Mystical Experience.
Even those who are liberated
Should have a drink of it."

20. There is nothing wrong
With the state of Liberation,
But the Nectar
Of Mystical Experience
Is so pure and sweet
That even the timeless state of Liberation
Yearns for a taste of it.

21. Every night there is a moon,
But only when it gets the unobstructed
Vision of the Sun
Does it become full
And shine its brightest.

22. A young girl possesses the bud of youth,
But only when she is united with her beloved
Does it blossom into flower.

23. Only when the Spring season arrives
Do the trees begin to kiss the sky
With their branches
Laden with fruit and flowers.

24. Likewise,
I am now serving the dessert
Of my spiritual attainment
In the form of this Nectar
Of Mystical Experience.

25. Some souls have attained Liberation,
Some are seeking Liberation,
And some others are still in bondage.
These remain different [in understanding]
Only so long as they have not tasted
This Nectar Of Mystical Experience.

26. Just as the streams
Which come to play in the Ganges
Become the Ganges,
Or as darkness going to meet the Sun
Becomes the light of the Sun;

27. Or as we may speak of different metals
Only so long as they have not been touched
By the philosopher's touchstone,
Which turns them all to gold;

28. So, those who enter deeply into these words
Are like rivers which, mingling with the ocean,
Become one.

29. Just as all possible sounds
Meet in the sound, AUM,
So there is nothing else,
In all the universe,
But the Self.

30. It is impossible to point to anything
That is not God.
Truly, everything is Shiva.

31. Jnanadeva says,
"May everyone in the universe
Enjoy this feast of the Nectar
Of Mystical Experience.

* * *

HARIPATHA

Haripatha: Introductory Note

In addition to his major works, Jnaneshvari *and* Amritanubhav, *Jnaneshvar composed a number of devotional songs as well. In them, he sings of his inner experiences and of his love of God and his Guru, Nivritti. One such collection of songs is* Haripatha, *or "Sing The Name Of Hari," in which he utilizes a traditional poetic form to extol the practice of the repetition of the name of Hari, an endearing name for God. These songs, presumed to have been written during Jnandev's years at Pandharpur, are sung to various melodies in Maharashtra to this day, in their original Marathi.*

Many of the great saints of Maharashtra, Nivritti, Jnaneshvar, Tukaram, Namadev, and Eknath, wrote such Haripathas, *declaring the chanting or repeating of the name of God to be the simplest, easiest, and surest way to the continual recollection of God's presence. This practice is regarded, throughout India, as the means to the focusing of the mind in contemplation of God, and as the natural expression of the love of God. Jnaneshvar advocates it as well; he says, 'Chant within the name of Hari; your heart will melt with love. And that love will open the door to the true awareness -- that you and your beloved God are one.'*

HARIPATHA

I.

One who ascends, even for a moment,
To the threshold of God
Will assuredly attain the four stages of Liberation.
Therefore, chant the name of Hari --
Yes, chant the name of Hari!
The value of chanting His name is immeasurable;
So let your tongue eagerly chant the name of Hari.

The authors of the Vedas and the various scriptures
Have all proclaimed this path with their arms upraised.
Jnanadev says: chant Hari's name;
The Lord will then become your slave,
Just as Krishna became the servant of the Pandavas,
As Vyasa, the poet, has so excellently told.

II.

In all the four Vedas, Hari's praise is sung.
The six systems of philosophy, and the eighteen Puranas
Also sing Hari's praise.
Just as we churn curds for the purpose of getting butter,
Likewise, we churn the Vedas, philosophies, and the
        Puranas
For the purpose of tasting the sweet butter of Hari.
Hari is the goal; the rest is mere tales.

Hari is equally in everyone --
He's as much in all our souls as He is in the gods;
He's the inner Self of all.
Therefore, don't weary your mind with strange practices.
Jnanadev says: You will experience heaven
Just by chanting Hari's name.
Everywhere you look, you'll see only Him.

III.

This insubstantial universe, this web
Of interacting qualities (*gunas*),
Is but His superficial form;
His essence is the formless 'I'
Which is always the same,
Unaffected by the interplay of the qualities.
If you discriminate in this way, you will understand
That the continual remembrance of Hari
Is the supreme goal to be attained.
Hari is both the Formless and the changing forms;
Remember Him, lest your mind wander idly away.

He, Himself, has no form;
He cannot be seen.
He cannot be bound to a single form;
He's the Source of all forms,
Both the animate and the inanimate.
Jnanadev says: Rama-Krishna, the Lord,
Has pervaded my mind;
He is all I meditate on.
Blessed is this birth!
I seem to be reaping infinite fruits
From the good deeds I performed in the past.

IV.

To speak of performing strenuous deeds
When all one's strength is spent
Is nothing but foolish talk;
To speak of one's love for God
When there is no feeling in the heart
Is also worthless and vain.
Only when true feeling arises
Can love for God bear fruit.
Will the Lord appear to you at your sudden call?
No. You must yearn for Him in your heart!

It's sad to see that you weary yourself
With so many worthless tasks.
Day after day, you anxiously fret
For your petty worldly affairs.
My dear, why do you never think
To turn to Hari with love?
Jnanadev says: It's enough
If only you chant His name;
At once your fetters will fall.

V.

You may perform the rites of sacrifice,
Of follow the eight-fold path of yoga,
But neither will bring you to peace;
These are only tiresome activites of the mind,
And usually bring only pride.
Without true, heart-felt love for God,
You'll not attain knowledge of Him.
How is it possible to experience union with Him
Without the Guru's grace?
Without the discipline of sadhana, He cannot be attained.

In order to receive, one must know how to give;
Give your love, and He'll shower you with grace.
Is there anyone who would be intimate with you
And teach you your highest good,
If you felt no love for him?
Jnanadev says: this is my judgement based on experience;
Living in the world is easy in the company of the saints.

VI.

When one receives the grace of a saint,
His ego-consciousness dissolves;
Eventually, even God-consciousness will dissolve.
If you light a piece of camphor,
It produces a bright flame;
But after a while, both camphor and flame disappear.
In the same way, God-consciousness
Supplants ego-consciousness at first;
But eventually,
Even the awareness 'I am He' dissolves.

One who comes under the influence of a saint
Has arrived at the gates of Liberation;
He will attain all glory.
Jnanadev says: I delight in the company of the saints!
It is due to their grace that I see Hari everywhere,
In the forest, in the crowds, and also in my Self.

VII.

Those who have no love in their hearts for God
Accumulate a mountain of sin
Which surrounds them like a diamond-hard shell.
He who has no love for God
Is totally deprived of love.
He who never even thinks of God
Is undoubtedly an unfortunate wretch.

How can those who are ceaselessly gossiping
Ever attain the vision of God?
Jnanadev says: That which lives
As the Self of everyone and everything
Is my only treasure.
That is Hari.
It is He alone I adore.

VIII.

If our minds incline us to the company of the saints,
Then we'll acquire the knowledge of God.
Let your tongue be ever chanting His name;
Let your hunger be ever for Him.
Even Shiva, who is absorbed in His own Self,
Loves to hear the repetition of God's name.
Those who single-mindedly chant His name
Will realize Him, and be freed from duality.
They'll revel forever in the awareness of Unity.

Those lovers of God who drink the nectar of His name
Enjoy the same sweetness that yogis enjoy
When their Kundalini Shakti awakes.
Love for the Name arose early in Prahlada;
Uddhava won discipleship to Krishna
Through his love of the Name.
Jnanadev says: The way of Hari's name is so easy;
Yet see how rare it is!
Few indeed are those who know
The infinite power of His name.

IX.

He has no knowledge
Whose mind does not dwell on Hari,
And whose tongue speaks of everything but Hari.
He is a miserable person
Who takes birth as a human
And yet fails to seek the awareness of Unity.
How could that person find rest in the name of Hari?

Unless the Guru sweeps away the sense of duality,
How could he who has no knowledge
Relish the sweetness of chanting God's name?
Jnanadev says: Repetition of the Lord's name
Is really a meditation on Him;
By chanting Hari's name,
All illusion is dissolved.

X.

You may take a bath
In the confluence of the three holy rivers;
You may visit all the sacred pilgrimage places;
But if your mind does not always rest
In the name of the Lord,
All your efforts are in vain.
He is very foolish who turns away
From remembrance of God's name;
When the soul is drowning in misery,
Who else but God will rush to its aid?

Valmiki, who is certainly worthy of respect,
Has proclaimed the value of chanting God's name;
"The Name," he says, "is the one trustworthy means
For salvation in all the three worlds."
Jnanadev says: Please chant Hari's name;
Even your children will be saved.

XI.

It is enough to chant "Hari" aloud;
In an instant all your sins will be burnt.
When a pile of grass is set ablaze,
The grass is transformed into fire;
Likewise, one who chants Hari's name
Becomes transformed into Him.

The power of chanting the name of Hari
Cannot be fathomed or gauged;
It has the power to drive away
All manner of devils and ghosts.
Jnanadev says: All-powerful is my Hari;
Even the Upanishads
Have failed to express His greatness.

XII.

Taking baths in various holy rivers,
Observance of vows, and other such outward trappings,
Cannot grant fulfillment,
If in your heart no faith or love exists.
My dears, it seems that you're needlessly engaged
In the performance of unfruitful deeds!
It is only by the path of love
That God may be approached;
There is no other way.

Give love to God,
And He will be as tangible to you
As a fruit in the palm of your hand.
All other means of attaining God
Are like the attempt to pick up liquid mercury
That's been spilled out upon the ground.
Jnanadev says: I have been entrusted
By my Guru, Nivritti,
With the possession of the formless God.

XIII.

Only when you have the continual experience of God
As equally existing in everyone and everything
Will you be truly established in *samadhi*. [1]
This experience is unavailable to one
Who is addicted to duality.
Only when the mind
Becomes illumined by the experience of *samadhi*
Will it attain perfect understanding.
There is no higher attainment for the mind than this.

When one attains to God,
All miraculous powers are also attained;
But of what use are these powers by themselves
Without the bliss of *samadhi*?
In such a case, they are only obstacles
To one's progress on the path.
Jnanadev says: I have become supremely fulfilled
In the continual remembrance of Hari.

XIV.

The Goddess of destruction will not even glance at you
If you chant fervently and unceasingly the name of Hari.
The chanting of His name
Is equal to a lifetime of austerities;
All your sins will fly away.

Even Shiva chants the mantra, "Hari, Hari, Hari!"
Whoever chants it will attain Liberation.
Jnanadev says: I am always chanting
The name of the Lord;
That is how I have realized my Self,
The place of supreme inner peace.

XV.

Let the chanting of Hari's name
Be your sole determination;
Throw away even the mention of duality.
But, alas, such mastery
In the awareness of Unity is rare.
First you must practice the vision of equality;
Only Hari must be seen everywhere.
In order to do this,
The mind and senses must be restrained.

When all these essential requirements are fulfilled,
One merges in Hari,
And becomes Hari, Himself.
Just as one solitary Sun
Manifests in countless rays of light,
One solitary supreme Being
Manifests Himself in all these countless forms.
Jnanadev says: My mind is fixed
On one unfailing practice:
The chanting of Hari's name.
Thus, I've become free of all future rebirths.

XVI.

It is an easy thing to chant the name of God,
Yet they are few who chant His name
With full awareness of its power.
Whoever has attained the experience of *samadhi*
By chanting His name
Has acquired all the miraculous powers as well.

If you unfailingly commit yourself
To chanting His name,
Then miraculous powers, intellectual brilliance,
And a disposition toward righteousness,
All will be yours;
Thus will you cross the ocean of illusion.
Jnanadev says: The Lord's name has become
Engraved upon my heart;
Because of this,
I see Hari, my Self, everywhere.

XVII.

By chanting the name of Hari and singing His praise,
Even one's body becomes holy.
By practicing the austerity of chanting His name,
One makes a home for himself in heaven
That will endure for ages and ages.

By chanting His name,
Even one's parents, brothers, and other loved ones
Will become united with God.
Jnanadev says: The secret of His name's infinite power
Was laid in my hands by my Guru, Nivritti.

XVIII.

One who reads the scriptures devotedly,
Who repeats Hari's name,
And keeps company with no one but Hari,
Attains heaven;
He earns the merit of bathing in all the holy rivers.
But piteous is he who chooses
To indulge his mind in its wandering ways.

He alone is blessed and fortunate
Who continues to chant the name of God.
Jnanadev says: I love to taste the name of Hari;
Every moment I am meditating on Him.

XIX.

The proclamation and command of the Vedas
And all the holy scriptures
Is "Repeat the name of Hari,
The supreme Lord, who is the Source of all."
Without the remembrance of Hari,
All other practices, such as rituals and austerities,
Are only futile exertions.
Those who have dedicated themselves
To remembrance of His name
Have found unending peace and contentment.

They have become enveloped in its sweetness
Like a bee who, in its search for honey,
Becomes enveloped in the closed petals of a flower.
Jnanadev says: Hari's name is my mantra;
It is also my formidable weapon.
Out of fear of this weapon,
The god of death keeps his distance
From me and from my family as well.

XX.

The repetition of God's name
Is the only treasure desired by His lovers
By its power, all their sins are destroyed.
The chanting of His name is equal
To lifetimes of performing austerities;
It's the easiest pathway to Liberation.

For one who chants the name of God,
Neither yoga nor the ritual of yajna is needed;
The injunctions of duty do not pertain to him;
He transcends all illusion.
Jnanadev says: No other practices,
Or rituals, or rules of conduct are necessary
For one who chants the name of Hari with love.

XXI.

There are no limitations of place or time
For the chanting of Hari's name.
Hari's name will save your family
On both your mother's and your father's side.
His name will wash away every blemish and stain.
Hari is the savior
Of all who have fallen into ignorance.

Who can think of a word adequate to describe
The good fortune of one whose tongue is restless
To chant the name of Hari,
The Source of all life?
Jnanadev says: My chant of Hari's name
Is always going on;
I feel that I have thereby made
An easy path to heaven for my ancestors as well.

XX.

There are very few who make the chanting of His name
An unfailing daily practice;
Yet, it is in this way that one may gain
The company of Hari, Lakshmi's Lord.
Chant "Narayana Hari, Narayana Hari,"
And all material happiness
As well as the four stages of Liberation
Will dance attendance at your door.

If there is no room in your life for Hari,
That life is truly a hell;
Whoever lives such a life will surely
Suffer hell after death as well.
Jnanadev says: When I asked my Guru
The value of the name of God,
Nivritti told me,
"It is greater than that of the sky above."

XXIII.

Some philosophers say that
The universe is made of seven basic principles;
Others say the number is five,
Or three, or ten.
When Hari is realized, He reveals that,
No matter what the number,
All those principles emanate from Him alone.
But let us not be concerned with philosopher's games;
The name of God is not like that.
It's the easiest pathway to approach to the Lord;
It involves no strain or pain.

Some speak of *ajapa-japa* [2]
As the practice that should be used;
This practice leads to a reversal of prana's flow.
To pursue this practice,
One needs much stamina and strength of will;
But the chanting of God's name with love
Is free of all such difficulties.
Jnanadev says: I'm convinced that a man lives in vain
If he does not resort to the Name.
That's why I continue to extol
The chanting of the Name.

XXIV.

The practice of japa, austerity, and rituals
Is futile without true purity of heart.
One must have the heart-felt conviction
That God lives in every form.
Please hold onto that conviction,
And throw away your doubts!
Chant aloud, "Rama-Krishna, Rama-Krishna,"
As loudly as you can.

Do not become conscious of your position and your wealth
Your family lineage, or your virtuous acts;
All these considerations produce only pride.
Hasten only to sing Hari's name with great love.
Jnanadev says: Hari pervades my mind and my meditation
I feel every moment that I'm living in Him.

XXV.

To Hari, the learned and unlearned are the same;
By repeating His name,
Eternal freedom is won.
The Goddess of destruction will never even enter
That home where "Narayana Hari" is sung.

How can we know His greatness
When even the Vedas could not explain Him?
Jnanadev says: This vast universe
Has turned into heaven for me;
Such luscious fruit has come into my hands
Only because I cling to His name.

XXVI.

O my mind, cherish remembrance of Hari's name,
And Hari will shower His mercy on you.
It is no great difficult chore
To chant the name of the Lord;
Therefore, please chant His name
With a voice that is sweet with love.

There is nothing greater or more uplifting
Than the chanting of His name;
So why should you wander on difficult paths,
Forsaking the sweet path of His name?
Jnanadev says: I keep silence without,
And keep turning the rosary of His name within;
Thus my japa is always going on.

XXVII.

There is no pleasure as sweet as His name;
All the scriptures declare
That it's the secret to be attained.
So do not spend even a moment
Without enjoying the nectar of His name.
This world is only a superficial play;
It is only an imagination, after all.
Without the remembrance of Hari,
It's only a futile round of births and deaths.

By remembering His name,
All your sins will go up in flames;
Therefore, commit your mind to chanting Hari's name.
Take the attitude of adherence to Truth,
And break the spell of illusion.
Do not allow the senses to bar your vision of the Self;
Have faith in the power of chanting His name.

Be kind, serene and compassionate toward all;
In this way,
You'll become the welcome guest of the Lord.
Jnanadev says: The chanting of God's name
Is the means to *samadhi*;
This, I swear, is true.
This wisdom was bestowed upon me
By Nivrittinath, my Guru.

* * *

CHANGADEV PASASHTI

Changadev Pasashti: Introductory Note

The following is a translation of the letter which Jnaneshvar wrote to the Yogi, Changadev (See Book I, p. 73). It contains in brief form the whole of Jnaneshvar's vision of Truth. It is full of compassion and love for Changadev, whom Jnaneshvar, throughout the letter, refers to as equal to and synonymous with the ultimate Reality, the Self. It is a rare and beautiful document, written in verse, which reveals the charming personality and flawless vision of a great being who had become fully and completely merged in and identified with the universal Self.

CHANGADEV PASASHTI
(LETTER TO CHANGADEV)

1. Salutations to the Lord of all, [1]
Who is concealed within the visible universe.
It is He who causes this universe to appear
And it is He who causes it to vanish as well.

2. When He is revealed, the universe disappears;
When He is concealed, the universe shines forth.
Yet He doesn't hide Himself, nor does He reveal
Himself;
He is always present before us at every moment.

3. No matter how diverse and varied the universe
appears,
He remains unmoved, unchanged;
And this is just as one would expect,
Since He is always One, without a second.

4. Though gold may be wrought into many ornaments
Its 'gold-ness' never changes;
In the same way, He never changes,
Though the universe contains so many varied forms

5. The ripples on the surface of a pond
Cannot conceal the water;
This universe of many forms --
Can it conceal His Being?

6. The element, earth, is not concealed
By the immensity of the planet, Earth;
Likewise, He is not concealed
By the immensity of the universe.

7. The moon above does not become hidden
By the glory of its fullness,
Nor does fire become hidden
By its leaping, roaring, flames.

8. It is not ignorance
That causes the separation
Between the perceiver and the perceived;
Truly, everything is Himself,
And He is the cause of everything.

9. Whether it is called a "shirt" or a "blouse,"
It is only the names that vary;
It is clear that both
Are only cotton cloth.
Though different kinds of clay pots
Are called by different names,
Their varied colors cannot conceal
The fact that all are made of clay.

10. The condition of separation
Does not exist in one whose vision is clear;
He remains alone, amidst all duality.
To him, the perceiver and the perceived are one.

11. Though different kinds of ornaments have different names,
All are made of gold.
Though a body possesses several different limbs,
Its unity is not disturbed.

12. It's the one pure Consciousness that becomes everything --
From the gods above to the earth below.
Objects may be seen as pure or impure,
But the ocean of Consciousness, ever pure,
Is all that ever is.

13. Though the shadows on the wall are ever changing,
The wall itself remains steady and immobile.
Likewise, the forms of the universe take shape
Upon the one eternal and unchanging Consciousness.

14. Brown sugar remains brown sugar,
Though it may be moulded into many forms;
Likewise, the ocean of Consciousness is always the same,
Though it becomes all the forms of the universe.

15. Various clothes of various patterns
Are made from cotton cloth;
Likewise, the varied forms of the universe
Are variously formed of Consciousness,
Which remains forever pure.

16. Consciousness always remains in its pristine state,
Unmoved by feelings of sorrow or joy;
Even though It may suddenly become aware of Itself,
Its state and Its unity remain forever undisturbed.

17. The world that is perceived comes into being,
And tantalizes the Perceiver within it;
Though even the rays of the shining Sun
Are but a reflection of Its own eternity.

18. From within Its own divine pure depths,
It gives birth to the perceivable world.
The perceiver, the perceived, and the act of perception:
These three form the eternal triad of manifestation.

19. In a spool of thread that's tightly wound,
Nothing can be found of the beginning or end;
The thread is so intricately bound
That its unity remains whole and undisturbed.
Without the triad of perceiver, perceived,
And the act of perception,
One pure and primal Consciousness
Enchantingly shines and sparkles alone.

20. Though It always has existence,
It sees Itself only when this 'mirror' is present.
Otherwise, there is no vision;
There is only the awareness of Itself.

21. Without causing any blemish in Its unity,
It expresses Itself through this triad as substance;
These three are the ingredients
In the creation of this perceptible universe.

22. When the perceived becomes manifest,
The perceiver comes into existence simultaneously;
And by what appears to be a substantial world
The eyes become beguiled.

23. When the perceptible world is withdrawn,
What can the eyes perceive?
Can the eyes have any purpose
If the objects of sight are not there?

24. It is only because of the existence of the perceived
That perception can exist at all;
If what is perceived is totally removed,
What food shall the other two have?

25. Thus, the three dissolve into absolute unity;
Then, only One exists.
The three exist in the void of imagination;
Only Oneness is real.
All else is a dream.

26. A face suffers no distortion
Until a mirror is brought;
Prior to that, its form and color are pure and true.
What a difference when it's reflected in a mirror!

27. Thinking that It's there within the mirror,
The Self reaches out to see Itself.
The eyes become thoroughly beguiled
When It confronts the image of Itself.

28. Before the world began,
It remained in Its own state,
Beyond perceiver and perceived,
Aware only of Itself.

29. Like sound, where there is no bugle or drum,
Or like fire, where there is no fuel to consume,
The Self, containing nothing in particular,
Remained pure and clear, in Its original state.

30. It cannot be spoken of or spoken to;
By no means may It be understood by the intellect.
It is always complete and whole,
And so It shall always be.

31. The pupil of an eye
Cannot see itself!
True, it is the very instrument of vision --
But it does not have such an ability as that.
In the same way, even the Self-realized Yogi
Is helpless to see the Seer.
Knowledge cannot know Itself;
The Perceiver cannot perceive Itself.

32. Where Knowledge is perfect and full,
Ignorance cannot exist at all;
So how could even the desire to know Itself
Arise in Knowledge absolute?

33. Therefore, one should address It
Through silence, by being nothing,
If one would be free, all-knowing, all-pervading;
For in that "nothing" all power exists.

34. It is stated in all the holy scriptures,
"One Reality remains ever steadfast;"
Like water within the curling waves,
That alone always remains.

35. It is Seeing, without an object;
It is Vision, clear, perfect, and free.
It exists alone, without anything else;
Within Itself is everything -- and nothing.

36. Its existence rests on non-existence;
It sees without any object to see.
It enjoys without any object to enjoy;
It is complete and whole in Itself.

37. Changadeva, you are a son of the Lord,
As a piece of camphor is a son of camphor.
O Changadeva, please listen to and heed
These words I'm uttering to you.

38. Jnanadeva says to Changadeva:
Your listening to my words
Is like my own hand
Accepting the clasp of my other hand.

39. It is like words hearing themselves being uttered,
Or like taste having a taste of itself,
Or like a ray of light hoping to give light
To other rays already bright.

40. It is like the attempt to improve gold
By mixing it with gold,
Or like a perfect face
Becoming a mirror in order to see itself.

41. Our conversation, O Chakrapani,
Shall be like that when we meet --
Like the attempt to see one's own self
By creating of oneself a mirror;
Or like sweetness
Trying avidly to taste itself.
Would its mouth not overflow with itself?
So also shall our mutual love.

42. O my friend, my heart expands with joy
At the very thought of seeing you.
But would it not be an error?
Would not our already perfect union wane and
die?

43. This desire of my mind to take such a form
As you and I meeting face to face
Arises suddenly in my heart with great warmth
of love;
But would it not debase our already perfect
union?

44. And in your heart, in your pristine, perfect,
state,
The will to act, to speak, or suppose,
Or not to act, to speak, or suppose,
Does not even arise. So you see, it's a
stalemate!

45. Changaya, in this pure name of yours,
There is neither action nor non-action.
What more can I say?
Surely, there is no 'I'-ness in you at all.

46. A grain of salt went to fathom the ocean's
depths,
But when it became immersed, where did it go?
What can it do and what can it measure
When it has altogether ceased to exist?

47. My plight is like the plight of that grain of salt;
Though I desire to see you, to play my role,
How and where shall I find you?
It is beyond my imagination to conceive!

48. Like one who awakes in order to encounter sleep,
And misses encountering it,
Here am I in order to encounter you
Who are completely pure and free like Nothingness.

49. It is certain that there is no darkness
In the light of the Sun,
And it is just as certain
That there is no awareness of 'I' in the absolute
Self.

50. Thus, when I embrace you in purity,
'I' and 'Thou' will swallow each other.
Truly, our meeting shall take place
When 'I' and 'Thou' are both devoured.

51. In the inner realm of vision,
The eye is able to perceive all sorts of images;
In this way it is able to see everything
Without moving from its place.

52. Likewise, when words arise,
Understanding tries to perceive their truth within.
It is in this place of inner vision that we shall see
The place where 'I' and 'Thou' both die.

53. Therefore, swallow altogether these limitations
Of 'I' and 'Thou', and we shall meet.
the pure harmony and joy of such a meeting
We shall surely relish always.

54. It will be like taste eating itself
For the sake of enjoying taste,
Or like an eye becoming a mirror
In order to see itself.

55. It is only by the 'words' of silence
that Nothingness becomes revealed.
It is with this garland of silent words
That I went forth, and thus enjoyed that perfect meeting.

56. Please understand the meaning of my words,
And thereby satisfy your hunger and your thirst.
Regard yourself as a shining flame
Burning brightly, without name or form.

57. These words are uttered simply
To open the eyes of your inner Self.
The perfect meeting with the Infinite
Is eternally within ourselves.

58. The rivers flow surely toward the sea,
but when the final Deluge comes,
Both rivers and sea are submerged.
In the same way, you should devour both 'I'
and 'Thou',
For, truly, you are the source of both.

59. Jnanadev says: You and I are one,
Without name or form;
We are identical to the one blissful Existence
In whom the blessed merge.

60. O Changaya, this knowledge has reached your doc
Unbidden, of its own accord.
Go now beyond both knowledge and what is knowı
And reach the final state.

61. O Changadev! My Guru, Nivrittinath,
Has spread this delicious feast for you
With boundless, motherly, love.
Please enjoy its sweetness.

62. Thus, Jnanadev and Chakrapani
Have met and merged,
Like two mirrors reflecting each other
In the eloquent silence that is Eternity.

63. If anyone were to read these verses,
Using them as a mirror to see themselves,
It's certain they would find
The pure and blissful Self of all.

64. Where there is nothing, what can one know?
The eyes can see, but can they see themselves?
How can knowledge be of use when all is oneself
To become one with the Self,
Surrender all the impulses of the mind.

65. Then you will know the 'sleep' beyond sleeping,
The 'awake' which goes beyond waking.
Now this garland is at last complete,
Fashioned of the word-flowers which Jnanadev
breathed.

* * *

About The Author/Translator

Swami Abhayananda was born Stan Trout in Indianapolis, Indiana on August 14, 1938. After service in the Navy, he settled in northern California, where he pursued his studies in philosophy and literature. In June of 1966, he became acquainted with the philosophy of mysticism through the teachings of Sri Ramakrishna, and experienced a strong desire thereafter to realize God. Abandoning all other pursuits, he retired to a solitary life in a secluded cabin in the mountain forests near Santa Cruz, California; and, in November of that same year, was enlightened by the grace of God.

He spent four more years in his isolated cabin, and subsequently met Swami Muktananda who visited Santa Cruz in 1970. Shortly thereafter, he joined Muktananda in India, at his ashram located not far from the region in which Jnaneshvar lived and wrote. His facination with Jnaneshvar grew with his visit to the saint's *samadhi* shrine at Alandi; and in 1976, following an inspiration, he created his English translations of *Amritanubhav, Haripatha,* and *Changadev Pasashti.*

In 1978, he was initiated by his master into the ancient Order of *sannyas*; and was given the monastic name of Swami Abhayananda, a Sanskrit name which means, "the bliss of fearlessness." Since that time, Abhayananda has taught the philosophy of mysticism and the art of meditation in a number of major cities throughout the U.S., and has lectured at numerous colleges and universities. At present, he resides in the Olympia area of western Washington state, where he continues to teach, write, and publish his works on the knowledge of the Self.

* * *

NOTES

AMRITANUBHAV

Invocation:

1. *Nivrittinath.* Jnaneshvar here uses the name of his Guru as a synonym for God. It literally means "Lord without *vrittis*," or mental modifications; i.e., the One in whom absolute stillness prevails.

Chapter One:

1. Verse 47: *Para to Vaikari.* In the philosophy of Shaivism, there are four levels of speech corresponding to the four bodies of man, each subtler than the one before. *Para*, the level of speech in which the initial thought-impulse originates, emanates from the perfect silence of the absolute Self. Passing through each level, that thought-impulse eventually manifests as gross speech, which is the final level called *Vaikari.* This subject is further elaborated upon in the Introductory Note to Chapter Three.

2. Verse 64: *Plantain tree.* The plantain tree, said to be hollow at its core, serves as a common metaphorical image to convey the idea of the identity of the inner and the outer, the individual soul and the universal Soul.

Chapter Two:

1. Verse 1: *sadhana.* Sadhana is synonymous with "spiritual practice"; including all endeavors toward Self-realization, like meditation, devotion, chanting, etc. One who practices sadhana is a *sadhaka.*

Chapter Three:

1. Verse 16: *Shiva Sutras.* According to legend, the *Shiva Sutras* were revealed to the sage, Vasugupta (9th century), who had a dream in

which Lord Shiva told him the whereabouts of a large rock on which Shiva, Himself, had inscribed some brief teachings regarding the nature of God, the soul, and the universe. These inscriptions, copied by Vasugupta, came to be known as the *Shiva Sutras*. Jnaneshvar's reference is to one of these aphoristic teachings (*Shiva Sutras, I.2): jnanam bandaha,* "[Relative] knowledge is bondage."

2. Verse 18: *sattva*. The reference is to *Bhagavad Gita,* 14.6: "...Sattva binds one to earthly joys and lower knowledge." According to Krishna, *sattva,* even though it is the best of the three qualities (*gunas*) of Nature, nonetheless mires one in the pleasures of the phenomenal world and intellectual knowledge. It is only when one transcends all the qualities of Nature in the experience of the absolute Reality, the Self, that one attains absolute Knowledge.

Chapter Six:

1. Verse 22: *ignorance*. By "ignorance" (*ajnana* or *avidya*), the Vedantic scriptures refer to that primary veil of unknowing which conceals from the individual his true nature as the eternal Self. Jnaneshvar argues that this "ignorance" is a phantom, existing only as an absence of knowledge; and, since it is itself an absence, it is not something that can be dispelled or destroyed. It ceases to exist simultaneous with the arising of knowledge, just as darkness ceases to exist simultaneous with the Sun's rising; it is not a 'something' which one can engage in any way.

2. Verse 28: *Agastya*. Reference is to the warrior-sage, Agastya, who, according to Puranic legend, had such a capacity for ingesting water that he once drank up an entire ocean.

NOTES

Chapter Seven:

1. Verse 165: *superimposition*. Here again, Jnaneshvar is addressing the Vedantic philosophers who uphold the view that the world is a "superimposition" on Brahman, the Absolute, just as a snake might be superimposed on a rope seen lying on the road. Jnaneshvar shows up the confusion inherent in this line of thinking. It is not that the Self is being overlaid by an imaginary image, or that something is being seen in it that is not there; the Reality is One. It appears as multiplicity to the senses simply because that's the way the Self appears to the senses. When we perceive the world, we are perceiving the Self; nothing is added or superimposed.

HARIPATHA

1, Chapter XIII: *samadhi*. *Samadhi* is synonymous with the mystical experience, or revelation, of the Self. It is that which Buddhists call *nirvana*, Sufis call *fana,* and Christians call "the vision of God." Usually, *samadhi* is used to refer to that rare and brief experience of the Transcendent obtained through profound meditation or devotion; here, Jnaneshvar is using the term to denote a continuous state of Self-awareness, the perfect establishment of the mind in uninterrupted God-awareness, whether in meditation or in one's normal active state in the world.

2. Chapter XXIII: *ajapa-japa*. *Japa* is the practice of the repetition of God's name; *ajapa-japa* is that repetition of God's name which requires no repetition. It is rather a listening to the breath as it comes in and goes out, with the awareness, *So-ham* (*sah-aham*, "I am That"). As the breath comes in, it makes the sound, *Sah;* as it goes out, it makes the sound, *Ham*. In the juncture where *Sah* gives rise to *Ham*,

and in the juncture where *Ham* gives rise to *Sah,* one may realize the stillness from which all sounds arise. According to certain Yogic texts, it is in this state of equilibrium that the Self may be realized.

CHANGADEV PASASHTI

1, Verse 1: *Lord of all.* In the original Marathi language, Jnaneshvar addresses Changadev as *Sri Vateshvar,* which is both a nickname of Changadev and a name for God. His intention is to raise Changadev immediately to the status of the pure Self, thus uprooting his identification with the limited form.

INDEX

A

B

C

INDEX

INDEX

H

I

J

K

INDEX

INDEX

INDEX

INDEX

T

U

INDEX